The Moray Golf Club at Lossiemouth
1889 ~ 1989

by

JOHN McCONACHIE

Printed and Published by
MORAVIAN PRESS LTD.
31 SOUTH STREET ELGIN MORAY IV30 1LA.
1988

James Mackenzie, Professional, with the class of 1955

To Hugh Tennant with all good
wishes.

John McConachie

Lossiemouth

Moray 2004

For Elizabeth and Neil

PREFACE

The history of a golf club is closely linked to its origins and to the area in which the club is situated, and even the golf club might be said to mirror the changes in society around it. The Moray Golf Club at Lossiemouth originated in the late Victorian and Edwardian period when seaside holidays, with the added attraction of a fine golf links, became popular, and the railway had brought distant parts of Britain within reach of the more adventurous of the propertied and middle classes.

Some of the events described at length took place a long time ago, but they may help to shed more light on a story which has become part of the folklore of Moray. With the authority and assistance of the Council of the golf club I have made full use of the carefully kept minutes of the times and I have relied on local and national newspapers and other sources to fill in any gaps in my knowledge. For any mistakes I alone am responsible.

My thanks are due to Mike Seton and his staff in the Elgin library, the staff of the British Library Newspaper Library at Colindale, and to Mrs Jane Cox and the staff of the Public Record Office at Kew for their assistance. Dr David Hamilton, Director of the Wellcome Unit for the History of Medicine at the University of Glasgow, read the manuscript at every stage and offered much valuable advice. Laurence Viney, editor of the *Golfer's Handbook,* and R.A.L. Burnet, historian and librarian of the Royal and Ancient Golf Club at St Andrews, were also very helpful.

Alister MacDonald, Mrs Sheila Lochhead, and Mrs Joan MacKinnon, the surviving son and daughters of Ramsay MacDonald, kindly gave me permission to quote freely from their father's papers and letters. I also wish to thank Mrs Hilda Cameron Marr, Mrs Norma [Glennie] Grant and Alexander Dunbar for allowing me to use letters written by their relatives to Ramsay MacDonald.

I am indebted to Bryan Pennington who took many photographs with his customary flair and cheerfulness and to Douglas Grant who was a sympathetic and imaginative publisher. My wife's continuous encouragement saw the history finished.

First published 1988
Second edition June 1990
© John McConachie 1988
ISBN 1 870151 01 1

Reproduction of the photographic prints on pages 8, 13, 16 and 58 by courtesy of the
George Washington Wilson Collection, Aberdeen University Library.

Photographic prints on pages 56 and 91 by courtesy of the
St Andrews University Collection.

CONTENTS

INTRODUCTION

by

Alexander Dunbar of Pitgaveny

The honour of introducing this excellent book has been given to me because the Stotfield links have been owned by my kinsmen for over 200 years, and it was my grandfather's uncle who, 100 years ago, leased to the Moray Golf Club that tract of untamed dunes which today forms the larger part of two modern golf courses.

John McConachie, an Aberdonian who has lived and practised medicine and golf in Lossiemouth for nearly 40 years, has unrivalled knowledge of the Club, the town and surrounding area. More than that, he has his finger on the pulse of social history, and has used his diagnostic skills on the personalities involved. He has brought the Club's history to life with tact, wit and flair. The story he tells is as palatable as the medicine prescribed - six hogsheads of single malt whisky a year.

Since it is part of the Club's history, he has rightly recounted in some detail the unhappy saga of a Prime Minister, himself born in Lossiemouth, whose membership was ended for the wrong reasons and re-instated too late to bring credit to anyone.

But this fascinating tale should not distract us from the main purpose of the book: to celebrate the game of golf and the Club which has nurtured it for 100 years. Blessed with a superb site beside the sea, with distant views across the Moray Firth and spectacular sunsets over Northern hills, the Club has not only survived two World Wars and an ever-expanding airfield nearby, but also provided for its members and guests rich refreshment for body and spirit.

It is the Centenary of the Club, and the fellowship induced by golf, humanity and nature, which this book celebrates, and I commend it warmly to all who hold golf and Moray dear.

Alexander Dunbar

The Moray Golf Club at Lossiemouth
1889 ~ 1989

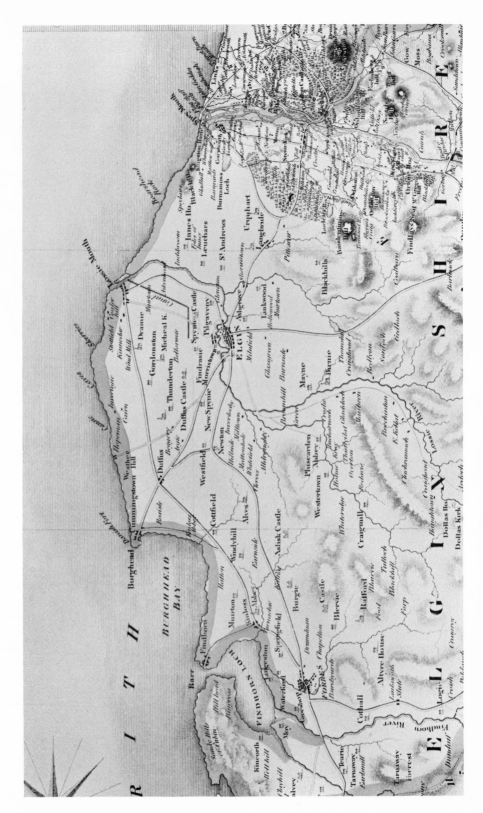

xii

The Early Years

THE MORAY GOLF CLUB at Lossiemouth was formed in 1889 at a time of great enthusiasm for golf throughout Scotland. An earlier attempt to start a club, which was recorded in a minute of 2nd April 1875, ended in failure after some years, although it is known that golf was played on open land to the east between James Street and the present clubhouse. The club which became defunct was also called the Moray Golf Club and its members played on a seven-hole course laid out at Stotfield on the ground between the house called The Camp and Skerrycliff. The first meeting to elect office-bearers of the new club was held on Wednesday 13th March 1889 in the Assembly Rooms, Elgin, home of the Trinity Lodge of Freemasons, and presided over by the Rev. Alexander Lawson. The chairman announced that the members of the club would play at Stotfield links where a course of sixteen holes had been secured.

In the event, the club was formally opened on 30th March 1889 with 82 members of whom about 50 were playing members. Of these, 30 members were solicitors, bankers, doctors and ministers, and the last group had increased to 10 by 1892 although they were outnumbered by the 20 solicitors. Apart from John Adam of Coulardbank, John Ferguson, Dr R.A.Miller and the treasurer, banker John Rodger of Lossiemouth, all the others were from Elgin. It continued to be a club for Elgin gentlemen, and later, English and London gentlemen and their ladies, and this is reflected in the constitution and the officials of the club until the end of the second world war. The membership of the Moray Golf Club in the early years included a number of distillers, some of whom played a very prominent part in the affairs of the golf club, and as will be seen, the effects of their vision and foresight continue to be enjoyed by members to the present day.

Golf before the Club
There is evidence that golf was popular in the Elgin area long before the formation of a golf club. David Hamilton, in *Early Aberdeen Golf,* suggests that golf was probably one of the sociable sports played on Sundays when people gathered from afar to attend church. According to Hamilton, the Reformation in 1558 brought in new, severe attitudes to sport in Scotland and sought to abolish sport on Sundays, at least at the time of the church services.

In *The Records of Elgin 1234-1800,* under "Church -Kirk Session" the following entry appears for January 19th 1596. "Walter Haye — comperit

Walter Hay, goldsmith, accusit for playing at the boulis and golff upoune Sondaye in the tym of the sermon, and hes actit himselff fra this furthe under the paynes of fyve lib. nocht to commit the lyik outher afoir or eftirnone the tym of the preaching." On February 28th 1649, "George Watsone, gouffer, burges of Elgin, wes decernit to mak payment to Alexr. Geddes, Skinner, burges ther, of four pounds 4s. money and that in contentione of certaine golf clubs coft and receawit be him fra the said Alexander".

Walter Hay and George Watson got off lightly in comparison with John Nauchtie in Mosstowie on April 11th 1602. In his case the Kirk Session ordered him "to pay 40s. of penalty and to stand three days in sackcloth for prophaning the Sabbath daye by plowing and harrowing; sawing of his cornis and threshing". Far from playing golf, the poor fellow was only going about his lawful business. As for the church elders who sat in judgment — on October 9th 1604 "Maister James Gairdin declairit that thair were certaine elders at the golf playand on Sonday last quha haid promeisit amendment".

Eighteenth Century
There is more evidence of golf being played in the eighteenth century in the Elgin area at Linksfield on the north-east border of the town, on land lying midway between the city and the palace of Spynie. This was the first move towards more open links land with its characteristic hillocks and scattered whins, and it is not surprising that the golfers finally set their sights on the long stretches at Lossiemouth. This adds weight to Hamilton's suggestion that "it may be that the players who were denied their game on the flat green round the church moved instead to the remote links outside the town to play their sport, with less chance of public scandal, detection or censure". The value of the links land on which golf was played at Elgin was soon appreciated, and about 1760 it became the farm of Linksfield. There is little mention of golf in Moray for over a hundred years but it seems unlikely that the golfers had given up — they had simply learned the art of discretion.

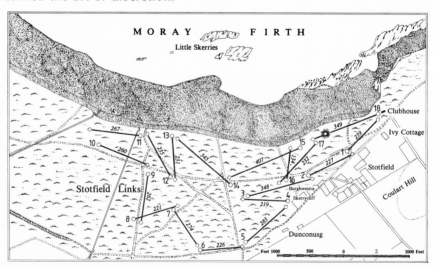

The Moray Golf Course — 1894
(From a Plan by W. Monro MacBey, Land surveyor, Elgin)

2

Land was leased at Stotfield from Captain James Brander Dunbar Brander of Pitgaveny, Patron of the club and one of the founder members, and sixteen holes were constructed in early 1889 by the contractor Stewart of Forres to a plan later approved of by 'Old Tom' Morris, the St Andrews professional. He inspired the pioneers to go ahead with his usual encouraging words — "Have nae fears, this will mak' a gran' course, or I've never seen ane." The formal opening took place on Saturday 30th March 1889 when the Rev. Alexander Lawson, captain of the club, briefly alluded to its formation and thanked Captain Dunbar Brander of Pitgaveny for his kindness in granting the use of the links, and asked him in the name of the members to strike off the first ball from the tee. Captain Dunbar Brander, in reply, stated that he was only too glad to do all he could for the good of the club and hoped it would have a prosperous career. He then struck off the first ball, which was greeted with a good ringing cheer by those assembled, and was then asked by the members to accept the golf club as a memento of the occasion.

Professor Alexander Lawson

Within twelve months the course had grown to eighteen holes, and on December 5th 1891 the young J. S. Urquhart established a remarkable green record of 78 in a club competition. The professional record was set at 71 early in 1892 by Andrew Kirkaldy. Oddly enough, several publications state that the previous lowest scratch score in a club competition — 87 — was recorded by the Rev. Alexander Lawson, on September 16th 1887. At the annual dinner of the Moray Golf Club held in the Station Hotel, Elgin, in December 1891, Lawson was referred to as the founder of the club and mention was made of his authorship of *Letters on Golf, by a Parish Minister,* published in 1889. He was a graduate of the Universities of Heidelberg and St Andrews and collegiate minister of Elgin in 1882.

The site was ideal with the fine springy seaside turf of links land and the beautiful view across the Moray Firth to the hills of Sutherland and Caithness with Covesea lighthouse in the foreground. Members of the golf club have thought for many years that this view was immortalised by a club member David West, R.S.W., artist and scratch golfer, on the cover of the famous Players cigarette packet, but this may be a local legend. David West's studio was on the fringe of the course, and he was to play a prominent part in club affairs for many years, but he was not one of the earliest members as he had not yet returned from the Klondike gold rush in the Yukon Territory of Canada. The clubhouse contains several fine examples of his paintings, which are eagerly sought after today, but he is best remembered by golfers as the man who invented and patented in 1907 the then modern tee box with extended legs which is still in use today

3

at the Elie golf club in Fife. The boxes had rests for bags of clubs and were quickly christened 'tee-caddies'.

Apart from David West, another club member was of an inventive turn of mind. John West of Letchworth Lodge, Lossiemouth, wealthy fish-buyer and curer, designed a peg tee whittled into carrot shape from the bung of a herring barrel, but unfortunately he omitted to patent his design.

Uniform of the Club.

The members of the Moray Golf Club were determined to be as sartorially elegant as those of other golf clubs and in 1899 the required uniform of the club was a scarlet coat with dark green collar and facings and brass buttons with the initials M.G.C.. Scarlet coats had been worn for ten years but the collar, facings and buttons were new.

Ladies were as eager as gentlemen to play golf on the new links and by 1897 there were 85 lady members, representing over one quarter of the membership. The ladies were kept firmly in their place by the Council who decreed that they should not commence play before 10.30 and that lady players, and gentlemen playing with ladies, whether going the full round or not, should allow gentlemen players to pass them. Nevertheless, the Council allowed the ladies access to the clubhouse from the start and indeed made special provisions for them.

Club competitions began when the twelve o'clock train on Saturday — later the one-fifteen — arrived from Elgin at the railway station on the bank of the river Lossie just beyond the Seatown. From there it was ten minutes walk to the links at Stotfield, but late arrival of the train resulted in more than one problem for members, as the secretary was wont to make the draw and start the competition at the advertised time. After a vigorous protest by some disgruntled competitors who found Sir William Gordon Cumming's foursomes well under way when they arrived, the Council felt compelled to point out that "the particular method of locomotion which members may adopt for enabling them to attend club fixtures whether by railway or otherwise is entirely a matter at their own risk".

In the early days — 1893 — a club was formed to convey members in the summer time for the sum of 1/- from the City stables in Elgin in a Brake or a Wagonette which left at 7 p.m. and returned from the golf clubhouse, Stotfield, at 10p.m.. Eighteen holes of golf in less than two hours with time for a few drinks in the clubhouse was obviously the norm, as the journey from Elgin took forty-five minutes. Club meetings were held in the Wagonette on the way home and jolly affairs they must have been too.

The "Wagonette Club" minute book — 1893

Legal Matters

Whether or not it was the influence of the large number of lawyers in the club, threats of litigation and of interdict abounded. As holes were altered and lengthened the course spread across the Cooper ditch at the western boundary and in 1890 a second lease was arranged with a new landlord Sir William Gordon Cumming of Gordonstoun. Sir William had resigned his commission as a Lt. Colonel in the Scots Guards following the 'Baccarat Case' scandal — in which the Prince of Wales (later King Edward VII) was involved — and retired to his Morayshire estates.

Sir William and Captain Dunbar Brander were Patrons of the golf club and had been elected honorary members for their generosity over the years. Both were keen golfers and in 1900 Sir William was moved to write to the Council of the club complaining that Captain Brander had threatened to boycott him and his guests off the golf course. Shortly afterwards Messrs. Grigor and Young informed the club that an action interdict against Sir William by Captain Brander had been intimated but happily it seemed to end there.

In the same year the golf club instructed the secretary to have a petition for interdict ready for presentation to the Sheriff in the case of fishermen or carters spreading nets on the course to dry. Dr A. M. Cowie of Dufftown, feeling aggrieved over the half crown he felt he had been wrongly charged for one of his guests, wrote the Council to intimate that if the money had not been returned to him within seven days he would instruct his solicitors to recover it.

Captain James Brander Dunbar Brander of Pitgaveny — 1896

The Distillers

Passions were soon calmed however by the shrewd action of the Distiller members — who had been laying down Dailuaine whisky since the formation of the club — in changing to Glen Grant whisky. In 1900 the club purchased one hogshead (fifty-four Imperial gallons of whisky) of 1894 at 7/6 per gallon, one of 1897 at 5/- and two of 1900 at 2/6. This practice continues to the present day and five or six hogsheads of Glen Grant are bought annually and bottled for the club at ten years of age. Within recent memory the whisky was bottled on the club premises by the house committee and a bottle was sent to the Council for their approval, but this practice was abandoned as members of the committee engaged in the bottling process became increasingly overcome by the fumes given off by the whisky.

In an article in the *Observer* in 1987 it was stated that The Macallan was the only whisky that is 100% casked in sherrywood, and the novelist Kingsley Amis declared that if he could only have one whisky he would choose The Macallan — and the ten year-old. At regular intervals over the years the Moray Golf Club has bought oak sherry casks for ageing its Glen Grant. Caramel is not added for colouring and the light amber colour of the golf club whisky is the result of ten years in the sherry cask. Some years ago, for a number of reasons, the Council decided to start laying down Macallan and in a few years the club whisky will be the ten year-old Macallan single malt.

James G. Thom, the secretary, ended his minute of the Council meeting of 30th August 1968 in his own inimitable style. "In the course of the meeting the Council saw fit to absolve themselves temporarily from their onerous tasks and to pass the new bottling of Glen Grant whisky. This was done with relish and the Council were unanimous in their approval of the quality of the whisky ."

The Clubhouse

In November 1889 the minutes record, "Ivy Cottage as being more convenient, has been secured as a clubhouse for the members". Although Ivy Cottage stood close to the golf course, on a site adjacent to that on which the Stotfield Hotel would later arise, members were impatient to have their own purpose-built clubhouse. The foundation stone for the new building was laid by Mrs Brander Dunbar Brander in July 1892 and within a few months a substantial new stone-built clubhouse had been erected, with tidy surrounds and neat fences, facing south-west and standing on a commanding situation overlooking the golf course. It was declared open by Sir William Gordon Cumming on January 2nd 1893 in the presence of a large number of members — including the dominie, James MacDonald of the Schoolhouse, Drainie, himself a keen golfer. He may have been responsible for nurturing a love of golf in his eager young pupil and future Prime Minister of Great Britain, James Ramsay MacDonald. Built at a cost of nearly £600, the clubhouse contained a large club room, luncheon room, a hall and lavatories, besides a dwelling-house for the clubhouse keeper.

This was sufficient for the members needs in the first few years but the rapidly increasing membership — and particularly the number of ladies — forced the Council's hand and a greatly enlarged clubhouse with a ladies room and locker-room was erected on the same site in 1900.

The building was financed by a grand Bazaar held in the Town Hall,

The first clubhouse — 1892

Elgin, on 8th, 9th, and 10th August 1901 and opened on successive days by Principal A.M. Fairbairn of Mansefield College, Oxford, Colonel [Sir] George Cooper of The College, Elgin, and Colonel Sir Felix Mackenzie of Forres in the absence of the Right Hon. A.J. Balfour. A sum of £999:7/- was raised and covered a large part of the costs of the new clubhouse.

In 1923 the building was further enlarged with the aid of a generous gift of £2000 and a ten year loan of £4000 at 4%, both from Alexander Grant of McVitie & Price — a close friend of Ramsay MacDonald's and later to become Sir Alexander Grant, Baronet, — and this is essentially the same clubhouse which is in use in the present day.

Seaside Holidays

The Morayshire railway, between Elgin and Lossiemouth, was the first line to be laid north of Aberdeen and was opened in August 1852. The carriages were pulled by the famous 'coffee pots', so called because the engines carried their water supplies in a tank under the frame, and in action looked like bubbling coffee pots. A small hotel with a few bedrooms was built at Lossiemouth station in 1853 and the village began to be known as a seaside resort for the county of Moray. On June 4th 1875 *The Elgin Courant* carried the following announcement under the heading "Early Trains for Bathers to Lossiemouth".

> As in former years, the Morayshire Railway Company have arranged to run early trains to Lossiemouth during the summer months for those who like to have an early dip in the briny deep before commencing the business of the day. From June till the end of September the train will leave Elgin Station at 7 a.m. arriving at Lossiemouth at 7.20 a.m. and departing again at 8.30 a.m.. This will give an hour and ten minutes to the bathers — ample time for having the desirable bath.

In 1899 the Council responded to an application from the Police Commissioners of Lossiemouth for a subscription towards the fund being raised for advertising *Lossiemouth as a Seaside and Health Resort* with a donation of one guinea, little realising what a rapid return would result from such a small investment.

Holidays at the sea for the wealthier middle classes were established in the late Victorian period and an added attraction was a fine links golf course. Golf at the beginning of this century began to enjoy great popularity among those who could afford it and the appearance of the wound Haskell ball from America gave further impetus to the game. Compared with the solid ball the new ball travelled an exciting distance, which made the added expense worthwhile. The Stotfield Hotel, adjacent to the clubhouse, was built in 1895 by the enterprising William Christie of the Station Hotel, Elgin, to cater for the large number of visitors and golfers, and the Marine Hotel next door followed in 1903.

²37

STOTFIELD HOTEL
LOSSIEMOUTH.

THE above handsome and commodious Hotel, erected little more than a year ago, has been added considerably to during the winter months and has now accommodation for over 40 visitors.

Situated on a commanding position close to the first teeing green of the **MORAY GOLF LINKS,** it has a sea view from nearly every window in the Hotel. Besides its close proximity to the *GOLF LINKS,* the *PUBLIC BOWLING GREEN* and *TENNIS COURTS* adjoin the Hotel grounds. The beautiful stretch of sands extending to Covesea Lighthouse give ample and safe bathing facilities. Boats can be had under the charge of experienced boatmen, and the walks and drives to places of interest in the neighbourhood are numerous.

The Hotel is under the personal management of the Proprietor, who is also Tenant of the **STATION HOTEL, ELGIN,** and there is Telephonic communication between the two houses.

Fixed Tariff for July, August, and September, £3 3s per week.

PRIVATE SITTING-ROOMS, from 5s per Day.

BILLIARDS.   HIRING.

WILLIAM CHRISTIE, Proprietor.

In *Elgin Past and Present,* written before the First World War, H.B. Mackintosh had this to say of Lossiemouth.

> The popularity of Lossiemouth originated with its golf course, now so celebrated. The climate is milder than that of St Andrews and North Berwick in the South, more bracing than Nairn some twenty-seven miles to the West, and is one of the driest in Scotland, the average rainfall over a series of years being less than twenty-one inches. Having the sea on three sides there is almost always, even on the hottest summer days, an invigorating breeze, while the place escapes the severity of the open sea by the shelter of the Banffshire coast on the East, and the Caithness and Sutherland coasts on the North-West. There is a fine sandy beach on which bathing is safe at any state of the tide, for there are no currents, hollows, or masses of seaweed. Dressing boxes are provided. There are also baths on the shore. Warships are often stationed off the coast for weeks at a time and their proceedings are a source of unfailing interest.

By 1904 the influx of summer visitors to Lossiemouth from the rest of Scotland, England and particularly the London area, had increased the annual membership to over 500 of whom 135 were ladies. Many of the better-off visitors built large villas at Stotfield and occupied them for two or three months of the year. Some idea of the upsurge in popularity of the game at this time can be gained from the growth of golfing societies and clubs. In 1890, one year after the birth of the Moray Golf Club, there were fewer than four hundred in the United Kingdom, but by 1900 there were well over two thousand.

The initial sixteen holes had swiftly become a fine testing eighteen hole course but this proved quite inadequate to cope with the large numbers anxious to play golf in such a beautiful place. Such was the

MORAY GOLF CLUB

PLAN SHOWING COURSES

1 9 0 5 .

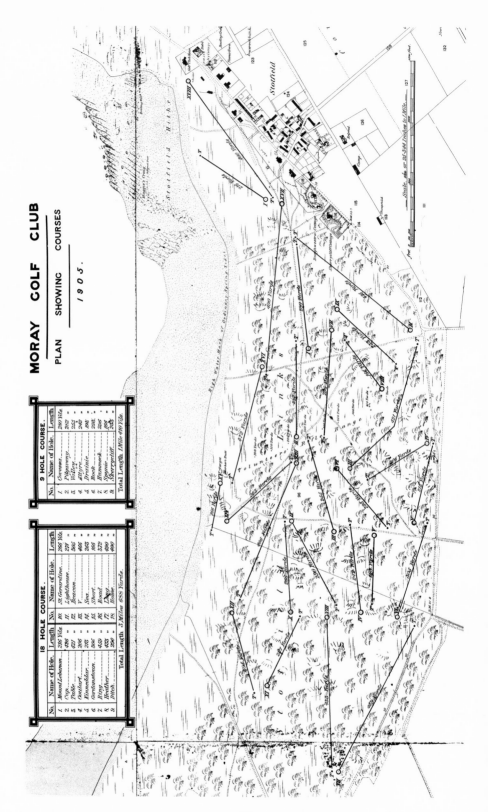

18 HOLE COURSE.					
No.	Name of Hole.	Length	No.	Name of Hole.	Length
1.	Mount Lebanon	366 Yds.	10.	St. Geraldine	366 Yds.
2.	Cup	486 "	11.	Lighthouse	297 "
3.	Table	321 "	12.	Beacon	366 "
4.	Contact	206 "	13.	V	383 "
5.	Kinneddar	291 "	14.	Sivec	393 "
6.	Gaitunstoun	366 "	15.	Short	161 "
7.	Ring	459 "	16.	Road	372 "
8.	Heather	433 "	17.	Long	490 "
9.	Ditch	290 "	18.	Home	400 "

Total Length 3 Miles 688 Yards.

9 HOLE COURSE.		
No.	Name of Hole.	Length
1.	Corseas	280 Yds.
2.	Pilgarway	282 "
3.	Valley	255 "
4.	Whyn	242 "
5.	Deerwick	193 "
6.	Rock	283 "
7.	Hammock	326 "
8.	Square	206 "
9.	Skerrycliff	203 "

Total Length 1 Mile 410 Yds.

10

demand during the summer months from July to September that by 1904 a starting sheet was in operation from 9 a.m. until 6 p.m., and a full-time starter — dressed in the uniform of the club — was engaged to supervise and start the golfers from the first tee. Apart from the large numbers of temporary members and visitors, 1903-4 saw the annual membership increase by 233 of whom over eighty were from the Edinburgh area and England, forty coming from London itself. This caused great congestion on the links and plans were drawn up for another course — a Relief course of at least nine holes, although eighteen holes were considered. Henderson and Stirk in describing Ben Sayers, the North Berwick professional, refer to "the hey-day of the Victorian and Edwardian era at North Berwick, when it became the most fashionable golfing resort in Britain". The golf resort of Lossiemouth, at least in the Edwardian era, cannot have been very far behind.

The Council found themselves in almost continuous session during the summer months and were forced temporarily to abandon their practice of holding their meetings in the secretary's office in Elgin and repair to the clubhouse at Lossiemouth if for no other reason than to deal speedily with the rush of applications for membership. The management of the club had been far-seeing enough to combine the offices of secretary and treasurer in 1898 and had appointed A.F. Macdonald, an Elgin solicitor, to the new position with the princely honorarium of twelve guineas.

In 1905 a new Ladies/Relief course of nine holes was built within the existing eighteen hole course, a sum of £1250 was earmarked for the upgrading of the clubhouse, the entry fee was to be raised to £2: 2/- and a request from the ladies for a wardrobe and a larger window for their locker room was looked on favourably. The proposal to raise the entry fee did not find favour and it remained the same as the annual subscription at one guinea. If the minutes of the day suggest that the Council were a somewhat autocratic body of men — for example the emergent Professional Golfers Association's repeated appeals for recognition and a donation were disdainfully allowed "to lie on the table" — at least they seemed to recognise that the ladies were unwilling to be relegated to the background.

The Northern Amateur Championship which had been inaugurated at Lossiemouth in 1894 and brought entries from all over the country continued to attract great attention from players and spectators, but even it had to yield to the press of members and summer visitors wishing to play golf in August. It was transferred to the month of September, and then to July without greatly affecting its popularity, although a prominent member of Council, Sheriff James Webster, was in favour of abandoning it altogether.

Nothing it seemed could disturb the long Elysium of golf at Lossiemouth, not even the Corporation scavengers who drove their cart and horse over the seventeenth green sparking off an angry correspondence with J. Hay Glennie the Town Clerk. Nor the letter from the same gentleman in his capacity as Clerk to the Drainie School Board — where the young James Ramsay MacDonald, soon to figure so prominently in the annals of the Moray Golf Club, had been a pupil — regretting that the dates for the school holidays could not be altered to provide caddies for the Championship. He went on to point out that, as the summer vacation was regulated by the leaving and returning of the fishing fleet, the effect of acceding to the request of the golf club would amount to the granting of extra holidays and the Board could not agree to the club's request.

This was just the beginning of an era of unrivalled prosperity for the Moray Golf Club which continued up to the outbreak of the First World War and after the horrors of that war, resumed in even greater measure until the Second War after which things were never to be quite the same again. This prosperity did not spill over into Lossiemouth itself except in a limited way with the local tradesmen and the Stotfield and Marine Hotels reaping a rich harvest, and the local inhabitants, whose menfolk earned a hard living on the sea, letting out their houses to the more prosperous of the summer visitors.

What were the attractions of Lossiemouth in those long forgotten days? The sun which set in January in the south-west set in midsummer almost in the north, and long lazy afternoons, warmed by the Gulf stream as it flowed around the north of Scotland and down into the Moray Firth, merged into long light evenings when golf could be played until almost eleven o'clock at night. This, allied to several miles of broad white sands, with the safest bathing of any seaside resort, and with perhaps that stillness and sense of timelessness the present generation of American professional golfers — embodied in Tom Watson and Ben Crenshaw — have discovered at Royal Dornoch further north contributed to a feeling of rest, recreation and well-being not to be found in the cities of the south.

Whatever it was it attracted Prime Ministers, Cabinet ministers, members of the aristocracy and the upper classes, and just the plain wealthy including E.M. Hutchinson, of the Mersey Flour Mills, Liverpool, who expressed an interest in buying the clubhouse for his summer residence but who eventually and happily lost interest. He might indeed have made an offer which could not be refused.

The present day profusion of cups and trophies, conservatively valued at over £30,000, is in contrast with the initial club prizes. Two medals were played for in 1889, the Town Council — or Corporation — medal (scratch), which was presented by the Elgin Town Council, and the Pitgaveny medal (handicap) donated by Captain Dunbar Brander. Both medals were last played for in 1923 and then disappeared. Captain James Brander Dunbar presented a new medal in 1924, the handsome Pitgaveny gold medal, and this is still played for annually and is now awarded for the best scratch score at the Autumn meeting.

Overseas members

In the days of Empire the club always had a large number of overseas members in every quarter of the globe. There is tangible evidence of this in the lounge today where a tall handsome Jacobean clock stands with an inscription in verse from the pen of 'H.B.' of *Punch,* who was himself an overseas member of the club.

Presented by the Overseas Members to The Moray Golf Club — 1927

By distant rough, lone bunkers, far-flung tees,
Man's laboured rounds the eighteenth green attain;
So we, the leave-men of the Seven Seas,
By devious routes this common harbour gain.

And here we set this tallyman of time,
Bidding him mark our minutes disappear
Less slowly in the far and alien clime,
Less swiftly — oh! less swiftly — when we're here.

The fourth (Skerrycliff) green in 1893. Note the barefoot caddie

The second (Rock) green in 1893

13

The Brighton of The North

A fulsome article extolling the virtues of the Lossiemouth golf course appeared in the *Daily Telegraph* of August 25th 1902 whose reporter observed "and in some respects it excels the more noted Fifeshire golfing centres".

Hard on the heels of this, in its edition of October 24th 1902, *Golf Illustrated* produced a spread entitled "The Moray Golf Course, Lossiemouth — A Favourite Northern Golf Resort" accompanied by numerous photographs of the club house and course. Little wonder that a member of the Moray Golf Club was moved to verse and the following appeared in *The Moray and Nairn Advertiser* of 28th February 1903.

BONNIE LOSSIEMOUTH.

A Tribute to Elgin's Health Resort.

Beside the Moray Firth there lies
A little seaport town,
Which only just is on the rise
To glory and renown.
Long years ago this health resort
Three 'cots' could only boast,
But now it is the finest port
Along the Scottish coast.

It has a stretch of golden sand,
It's got a fine hotel;
So if it only had a band
No place could it excel.
From grand machines drawn up in state
The bathers sally forth;
For now it's coming up to date —
The Brighton of the North.

A better golf course can't be found
Throughout the Empire wide;
That ditch and whin impede the round
By none can be denied;
But after all a sporting course
Is really far the best,
And be there ditch, or be there gorse,
It fairly licks the rest.

The smoking-room's a splendid view
of all the country wide,
The Moray Firth so calm and blue,
With fast receding tide.
The ladies' room is very trim
Although a little dark;
'Twas furnished by the wife of him
Who gave the Cooper Park.

The red-roofed church from far you see
It is so small and quaint,
It's called St Gerardine's, for he
Was Stotfield's patron saint.
From John o' Groat's to Solway Firth,
Or even further south,
You will not find a place on earth
Like bonnie Lossiemouth.

E.L. Galletly.

Elgin, 19th February 1903.

14

J.L. Low of St Andrews was a fine golfer who played for Scotland in 1904 and spent his golfing holidays at Nairn. He wrote notes for the *Athletics News* and in July 1903 the following extract occurred. "…. there appear to be difficulties in the way as to the cutting of bunkers, for Nairn is a prohibitionist place. Bunkers are difficult to obtain, and stronger drink than mineral water is not allowed to be vended in the club-house, so that every man must be his own wine merchant." The clubhouse at Lossiemouth with its large tumblers of whisky — cheaper than the gingerbeer — would have suited John Low.

The Bulger

On July 4th 1894 the first Lossiemouth edition of the newspaper *The Bulger* appeared, declaring itself to be *A Summer Journal For Lossiemouth, Elgin and Neighbourhood.* Naturally enough it contained an article praising the excellence of Lossiemouth as a health resort. The writer went on:

> The already famous golf course can hold its own with any on the eastern seaboard of Scotland. During summer and winter it is always dotted with players; but there is never the anxious rush, the drawing for places, the quarrel or discontent of the older links of St Andrews or North Berwick. There are always players on the green, yet all goes with a smoothness and good humour which speaks well for the organisation of the Club, and the civility of its members.

An advertisement for the Harbour Hotel intimated that "Visitors can depend upon being supplied with the choicest brands of Champagne, Wines and Spirits. Pleasure sailing and fishing parties arranged for." It seems unlikely that in 1894 there was much demand from the locals for champagne.

The Bulger carried a prominent announcement of the golf club's fixtures for July. On the 11th there was a "Sea Trip to Dornoch. Golfers and others leave Lossiemouth Pier at 7.15 a.m.. Tickets 5/- to be had at Club-House." The intrepid band set off in the S.S. Earnholm and a twenty-eight-a-side match ensued at Dornoch. Whether the crossing was too rough or the renowned hospitality at Dornoch too much we will never know — probably a bit of both. The Moray golfers were beaten by 237 holes to 1 hole. The S.S. Earnholm belonged to the Moray Firth Steam Fishing Company and had been used by the Dornoch golfers in the same way to visit Lossiemouth the previous year, but then it had been forced to sail into Burghead harbour as the harbour at Lossiemouth was being deepened at the time.

Caddies at the second clubhouse — 1900

16

CHAPTER II

The Caddies

C ADDIES played a prominent part in the Moray Golf Club scene from the outset. It appears from early photographs that almost as many men as boys carried, and the boys were frequently barefoot which must have been rather painful amongst the gorse. Until the beginning of the century it is obvious that golf bags were the exception rather than the rule, but it was not difficult to tuck four or five clubs under the arm and fewer clubs had to be cleaned at the end of the round. The boys seem to have been an unruly lot and exercised the Council greatly in their control.

Nuisances were frequently committed and even the provision of a urinal in 1902 did not seem to satisfy them. The clubmaster complained of the conduct of the caddies about the clubhouse grounds, the greenkeeper complained of stones being thrown on the last green and John Fraser of Lenniemore (now Hamewith) wrote irascibly of the injury done to his dyke by the caddies. His large garden bordered the 'slicers' side of the eighteenth fairway, and still does, and reaped a rich harvest of balls from wayward tee shots. He continued to write frequently to the Council expressing surprise that the club should refuse to recognise the damage done to his dykes "by members and caddies" but indicated that he would be agreeable that the hole in the corner nearest the clubhouse should be repaired as suggested in the secretary's letter.

David West the artist had a trying time in his studio at "Chilkoot" between bad language used by the caddies and the throwing of stones and rubbish into his garden. He wrote two letters of complaint to the Council in quick succession stating that he had the names of the boys and asked the Council to enquire if the caddie-master was attending to his duties. The secretary passed the letters to the Chief Constable and the Council promptly received another sharpish letter from West enquiring who had given him permission to do that.

An article about the golf club at Lossiemouth in the illustrated magazine *The King* on 26th August 1905 contained the following extract.

> The caddies are mostly the sons of Lossiemouth fishermen. Few of them play golf, or are of much use to the inexperienced player. They are generally a silent and unresponsive lot, whose conversational powers do not extend beyond a yes or no. They can at times, however, speak with brutal frankness, as one golfer found. He was playing in a mixed foursome and making a terrible mess of his game. He appealed to his caddie, and asked what he could do to play better. "If you want to play gowff," said the caddie, "dinna play wi' women." There was sound sense if little gallantry in the advice. On another occasion a player who was foozling stroke after stroke despairingly asked his caddie, "Shall I ever play golf?" and received the consoling reply, "Never."

Regulations of ten, and later, thirteen points were drawn up for organising the caddies and penalties were severe. "Caddies who commit a breach of any of the above regulations will either be suspended from carrying clubs for such period as the Council of the Club may direct, or be dismissed from carrying clubs altogether, and Struck off the Roll." The Council were soon receiving complaints that members and visitors were ignoring the regulations and a poor example was set by R.A. Johnston who appropriated another Johnston's (Capt. C.E. Johnston) turn at the tee and also his caddie, on the 10th of August 1903, although the bemused starter was unable to give the Council a clear idea of what had transpired.

In spite of his running battle with the Council over the caddies and the price of ginger-beer amongst other things, the good-hearted David West organised golf competitions for the caddies and provided the prizes. He was rapped over the knuckles on one occasion for not employing a caddie and, like the Klondiker he was, replied to the secretary as follows.

Dear Sir,

In reply to your letter of 18th, I beg to say that the boy whom I usually take to carry my clubs is *my private servant* and is not engaged by me as a Caddie. I think I am only doing a good turn by taking out my servant and leaving the caddies to others. As the Caddie Master entirely fails to provide caddies, I see no reason why a Member may not take out his own servant if all the caddies are already employed.

If the Council can point out any rule prohibiting me from taking a servant to carry my clubs I shall at once fall in with their decision.

I am, Sir,
Yours faithfully,
David West.

The caddies were by no means all high spirited young boys. Many girls caddied and many men were employed on a regular basis. Two of the caddies who were cousins, and gave their lives in the Great War, are commemorated by a plaque on the sun dial which stands on the slope above the eighteenth green. The simple inscription is there for all to read and reflect on in passing.

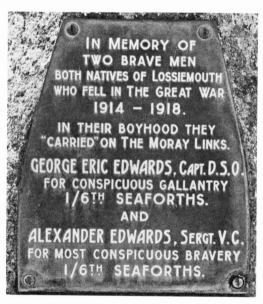

A number of older members still remember their caddie numbers and recall the well-known golfers, and particularly the professionals, for whom they caddied. Many golfers are recalled for their idiosyncrasies and many for their generosity. The Willock-Pollens spent the summer in "Firthside", their large villa at Stotfield, and H.C. Willock-Pollen's caddie recalls almost seventy years later how she was sent to buy herself a good pair of shoes at the end of each season she caddied for him. Mrs Willock-Pollen engaged a number of caddies for her family and took some of them to Elgin in her chauffeur-driven car to buy new clothes for them. John Foster as secretary was known as a martinet by the caddies and as soon as he appeared with his clubs to play golf they all took to their heels. The "Shooters" frequently deserted the grouse moors to play golf at Lossiemouth. There was never any shortage of eager and willing caddies on these occasions as the shooters — or "Shotters" as the caddies called them — were known to be liberal with their money, and word soon got around among those waiting when they arrived.

Caddie stories are still told with relish. "What's the Bogey here?" an elderly golfer asked his inattentive caddie at one hole. "Sevenpence ha'penny an ounce — Sir" came the quick reply. Or, "Where did that one go?" "Up in the air, Sir — but it'll soon be down." It should be explained that Bogie-Roll was black twist tobacco.

Iron clubs had to be cleaned at the end of the round and a good caddie always had his own emery paper, often two or three different grades. A preliminary rub with wet sand was followed by the vigorous use of emery paper, and the iron head finished off with a burnisher produced a mirror-like effect. Older caddies farmed out the rusted clubs of their employers to the nine and ten-year old caddies with the promise of a "fag" (a cigarette) for the best-cleaned club. Irons in those days had smooth faces without the deep grooves of the modern club. A well-cleaned club developed into an art form with shining vertical areas at the heel and toe and an equally shining horizontal area — the "sweet spot" — where the ball should be hit. Young Tom Morris once explained that it was particularly difficult to keep the eye on the ball when playing an iron shot by the unconscious tendency the striker had to let his eye follow the gleaming metal. Robert Harris of Carnoustie was one the earliest of the noted amateurs to play with black iron clubs, and Bobby Jones is reputed to have forbidden his caddie to clean the centres of his irons.

At the annual general meeting of the golf club in May, 1926, the captain responded to a question about the caddies and pointed out that they received 1/- a round with a tip over and above. He thought that 2/- for four hours with tips added was quite fair pay "for children of that age". From this and other references it is apparent that the better players took two hours for a round, but the poorer golfers could take up to two hours and a half. Much of the information on the cleaning of golf clubs was given to the author by Willie Cowie, who began caddying at nine years of age in the early 1920's and who recalls occasions when he carried clubs for four rounds in one day, although the fourth round was limited to twelve holes.

In the years of the depression, when the fishing industry at Lossiemouth was very badly hit, a considerable number of adults caddied along with the children and a regular income of sorts was made throughout the summer months. In many households the income made from letting the entire house to summer visitors helped to see the family through the winter. The family commonly retreated to alternative accommodation in the house or close to the house and offered some service to the visitors — although the more wealthy visitors brought their own servants. However, the Marine and Stotfield hotels were the normal habitat of families with servants. The people of Lossiemouth were a proud and hardy race and they took all this philosophically in the sure and certain knowledge that things could only get better. For many of them who had never had a golf club in their hands it made them determined that they too would one day play golf, and those who never played have continued to take a lifelong — and very knowledgeable — interest in the golfers on the links at Stotfield. One has but to witness the crowds at the Moray Open Tournament on a summer's day, or the eager spectators when Fred Daly, John Panton, Eric Brown or Harry Bannerman were working their magic in professional appearances over the Old course.

J.C. Thomson, John Panton and Jock Campbell after a round on the links.

Today the boys who would have been caddies in the past are members of the golf club, happily slashing their way around the New course carrying golf bags as big as themselves — and occasionally finding a lost ball in the impenetrable whin.

CHAPTER III

The Leases

THE two eighteen hole courses at Lossiemouth lie on land leased from the estates of Pitgaveny and Altyre until the year 2011. As it proved impossible to arrange a feu, the leaseholds were re-negotiated in December 1913 when the golf club was in its twenty-fifth year. This was no easy task and the Council of the club found the proprietors a little difficult to deal with.

Ernest Humbert, K.C., 4, Field Court, Gray's Inn, London, had a holiday home at The Camp, Dunbar Street, Lossiemouth, and was one of the oldest members of the golf club. He was also a close personal friend of the proprietors, Captain James Brander Dunbar of Pitgaveny and Sir William Gordon Cumming of Gordonstoun and Altyre, and this relationship was of great value to the Council in the delicate and prolonged negotiations.

When Captain Brander Dunbar succeeded his father as proprietor of Pitgaveny in 1902, two-thirds of the golf courses, as they were then, lay on his estate. Soldier, big-game hunter, forester and laird, the Captain, a somewhat unpredictable man, had led an interesting and adventurous life and was known to be the possessor of an unusual — at times eccentric — sense of humour. This is best exemplified by the fact that many years before his death he had a carpenter make a coffin from an oak tree on his estate and this was kept in the "coffin room" at Pitgaveny until it was required. The inscription on the brass plate read:

Pitgaveny: Born 1875.
A Fine Natural Blackguard.

He was not averse to showing his coffin to his friends, and this gave rise to a number of no doubt apocryphal stories. He gave a characteristically uninhibited interview to a reporter and a photographer from the *Scottish Daily Mail* some years before his death which appeared under the banner headline "Come and see my COFFIN says the old soldier", and was accompanied by a photograph of the coffin and the brass plate. Captain Dunbar's home at Pitgaveny contained one of the largest private collections of hunting trophies in the country which he described as representing "some damn fine shoots". He took part in the Boer War (1899-1902) and was a survivor of the siege of Kimberley in which Cecil Rhodes also took part. Known locally as "the Lairdie", Captain Dunbar was a colourful character who remained very active until his death in 1969.

He is remembered in Lossiemouth with some affection as a real character and tales about him still circulate.

In August 1912 the golf club had received several letters from Captain Dunbar and his agent calling on the club to fence the course in terms of their lease. Captain Dunbar also intimated that he would not allow the sale of spirituous or malt liquors in the clubhouse after 31st January 1913. This was a serious matter when one considers that the members drank 10,867 quarter gills of whisky at threepence a glass in 1912, and one can understand the feeling that his attitude was unreasonable and his demands should not be complied with.

News of this must have reached artist David West. He had complained of three caddies by name who had caused annoyance to him by playing golf near his house. When this complaint was investigated by the Chief Constable it was found that the boys were playing golf on the beach and not annoying West. This provoked a further letter from David West stating that as no stop was put to the annoyance by the caddies then he would bring up another matter in connection with the licence of the club. The golf club Council replied that they did not care for the threatening tone of his letter.

Over a period of many months of negotiations and numerous meetings, other demands were made and litigation was threatened by Captain Dunbar. The Council decided to obtain eminent legal advice with a view to resolving the problems raised out of court. The captain, J.H. Hair, with the secretary A.F. Macdonald, journeyed to Edinburgh at counsels' request to consult with James Avon Clyde, K.C., and William Chree, K.C.. The detailed memorial, with twelve questions and the considered answers of counsel, is carefully recorded in the minutes.

The lease contained restrictions on the erection of shelters and tool houses, and, in addition, Captain Dunbar interpreted it to empower him to warn off members of the golf club who displeased him. On one occasion he demanded that the golf club remove Sheriff James Webster's name from the list of members and stated that the club was bound under a £200 penalty to enforce the clause with regard to any member he might consider objectionable. When this demand was resisted he offered to cut down the warning-off of members to one per cent per annum. Later, his agent Law informed the secretary that, in the event of all other conditions being satisfactorily adjusted, Captain Dunbar was prepared to grant a lease at a rent of £100 and a grassum of £600, along with 10% of the net profits of the club by way of additional rent.

The new lease would not reserve right to the proprietor to turn off tinkers etc., nor would the club be bound to fence the course on the west. However, Captain Dunbar wished the club to undertake to remove from membership anyone who may have been grossly offensive to him and refund him any government duties payable in renouncing the present lease.

The Council would give no such undertaking. With regard to precedence on the golf course, Captain Dunbar and any friends *bona fide* living with him at Pitgaveny would have the privilege of the clubhouse and course, and the Captain and anyone playing in a match with him had precedence at the first tee. This privilege did not extend to the provision of free food and drink. A later request that similar privileges should be granted to Captain Dunbar's brother was acceded to, but the Committee refused to extend this right to the shooting tenant or tenants of Pitgaveny.

The negotiations with Sir William Gordon Cumming also presented some thorny problems, chiefly over the extra land the club considered should be leased for two full eighteen hole courses. Ernest Humbert wrote to the Council:— "I sent your last letter to Sir William Gordon Cumming who definitely declines to include the extra land in the new lease and his answer must be taken as final. Sir William does not think it would be fair on his successors to tie up this large area of land for nearly a hundred years and it is impossible to say that he is wrong."

In December 1913, provisional agreements were concluded with both proprietors for 98 years from Whitsunday 1913. The leases covered 122 acres on the Pitgaveny estate and 120 acres on the Gordonstoun estate with a grassum of £650 and an annual rent of £100 for the former and a grassum of £325 and rent of £50 for the latter. The Council must have heaved a collective sigh of relief.

Captain Dunbar's ambivalent relationship with differing personalities was later seen in his running battles with the Lossiemouth Town Council, particularly over the town square. The square had been gifted to the town by his father in 1897 but the Laird — who apparently retained rights as the superior — strongly disagreed with the Town Council's proposals for its use. In 1928 Captain Dunbar had prevented the Council from allowing the square to be used for circuses. In 1929 the Council retaliated by refusing to allow the Captain to build houses on the square. In 1932, he demanded that the Town Council remove a notice prohibiting lorries from crossing the square, but the Council chose to ignore the demand. *The Daily Express* interviewed Captain Dunbar.

I put an axe in my car, he said today, and, after calling on the town clerk and informing him what I proposed to do, I went to the square to hack the board down with my own hands. I found, however, that the board was not erected, as I supposed, by itself, but was fixed to a telegraph pole clear of the square. That altered things, and I decided not to use the axe. It was then that the ploughing idea was hatched.

Early one morning in April 1932 he sent his grieve from Oakenhead farm to Lossiemouth with a plough and two horses with instructions to plough up part of the square. Before a crowd of interested onlookers, including the police sergeant, three long parallel furrows were cut on the west side. Shortly afterwards he announced that it was his intention to hold a ploughing match on the square for which he would donate prizes. Naturally enough an Elgin poet broke into verse and the local paper duly obliged. The first verse will suffice.

Hae ye heard hoo the laird
The puir cooncil has scared,
An' left them a' fair in a stew, a stew;
For fat has he deen
But turned up the green,
An' furrit the square wi' a ploo, a ploo,
An' furrit the square wi' a ploo.

Shortly afterwards the Captain dropped another bombshell on the Town Council in order to demonstrate his ownership of the town square. *The Northern Scot* carried an extract from an article in a daily newspaper which had appeared with the Captain's authority.

In a perfectly friendly frame of mind, but by way of bringing the Council to a more speedy realisation of where they stand than the proposed ploughing match is calculated to achieve, I had provisionally planned for last weekend the interment of an unclaimed

23

"We'd raither hae a circus!"

inmate from the most accessible asylum. The corpse was to have been buried in the Square just opposite ex-Provost Cormack's house. Meantime I am marking time — in all good humour, but in absolute sincerity. The ploughing match or the sepulchre or both are not shelved, but merely postponed. The Town Council cannot be allowed to go on perpetuating this strife, for it is detrimental all round, and they must be brought to heel. When this burial takes place they will require an order from the Home Office to exhume the remains. Even then they will have to treat with the estate over the removal of the tombstone or the alteration from "lies" to "lay the mortal remains of Count _____ ".

A *Northern Scot* reporter interviewed several members of the Lossiemouth Town Council who were inclined to treat the matter as a huge joke. Ex-Provost Cormack said he had retired from municipal life. When asked if he thought Captain Dunbar would carry out his threat he replied, "Nobody knows what the Laird will do next". Councillor Allan MacLean asked the reporter if the proposed corpse was that of any relation of Captain Brander Dunbar. "I think," he continued, "that it is extremely bad taste, especially for a man of his social position, to suggest that a poor creature who was afflicted with a trouble of that kind should be interred there. But at the same time, if there were such an interment, a very fitting companion would be Captain James Brander Dunbar."

Provost Smith said "the whole thing is piffle, and just another attempt by Captain Brander Dunbar to keep the ball rolling. He is not a bad fellow you know. We (the Council) will be very disappointed if we do not receive a funeral letter inviting us to the burial, and I would be glad to officiate at the graveside in the absence of a minister."

Councillor Tulloch said he regarded it as "a lot of tripe" and Councillor Gault stated that if the Laird was going to act like a fool the Council would not stand in his way. When informed that the Council refused to take his threat seriously, Captain Dunbar asked — "Then you do not think they are going to do anything about taking the ground over from me? Very well then, I will just have to go down and see about howking a hole. I have not threatened the Council at all, but have merely stated that to vindicate my rights on the Square I have arranged to plant a body in it."

The report continues — "Following the charity football match at Elgin at which he and Provost Smith officiated as linesmen, Captain Brander Dunbar, accompanied by employees on his estate, motored to the Square at Lossiemouth. Armed with iron spikes they proceeded to dig these into the ground as if to ascertain the best part of the ground for the interment. During this procedure the Laird was heard to remark to an employee, "I am saying, Wullie, a burial will be a new job for you".

As with the golf club, an amicable settlement was eventually arrived at without the necessity for ploughing match or burial.

London Members

Many members of the Moray Golf Club were accustomed to London clubs where they could while away Sunday afternoons without the distraction of wife or family, and repeated requests for the opening of the smoking-room of the clubhouse on Sundays were made to the Council over the years. The first request was made in 1906 and eventually James Terry of London was invited to put the case for the members at a Council meeting in August 1921. He felt that it was exceedingly dull at Lossiemouth on Sundays and that visitor members who were used to clubs which were open on Sundays would find it a great boon if they were at liberty to use the smoking-room on a wet and windy day. The Council's reply was that the constitution of the club did not permit them to open the clubhouse on Sundays. A later request, signed by a number of the London members, was put to the Council in August 1923.

Dear Sir,

We, the undersigned members, request that the lounge of the clubhouse be opened on Sundays during August and the half of September from 2 p.m. until 7 p.m. for the use of members only, — lady members and visitors not to be admitted. It is understood that no refreshments of any description are to be served.

(sgd.) Walter Shakespeare, Lewis Noad, Ernest Humbert, D.C. Blair, James Terry, A.W. Mitchell, A.R. Cumming, C.A. Tomes, H. McMichael, E.C. Hardwicke, John H. Perry, J. Herbert Fisher.

As on previous occasions the Council was of the opinion that the granting of the request was *ultra vires,* and those members who were bored by six weeks of Sunday afternoons in Lossiemouth had no other course than to lump it. However, after a little more discreetly applied pressure, the matter was duly brought up at the next annual general meeting in the form of a motion which won the necessary support and the clubhouse was opened on Sundays the following year. No doubt the matter of refreshments was readily solved with a little ingenuity.

CHAPTER IV

The Moray Golf Club and the Prime Ministers

FOR entirely different reasons the two members who figure most prominently in the history of the club are Herbert H. Asquith, Prime Minister from 1908 to 1916 and later Earl of Oxford and Asquith, and James Ramsay MacDonald, M.P., a son of Lossiemouth who was not to become Prime Minister until 1924, and for a second time from 1929 to 1935. The first was attacked physically while enjoying the pleasures of the Moray golf links: the second was attacked by a body of influential and determined members in a much more subtle and unpleasant manner than by hitting him over the head.

Herbert Asquith married Emma Alice Margaret Tennant — always known as Margot — daughter of Sir Charles Tennant Bt.. Margot's brother, Francis Tennant, the second son, divided his time between his homes in North Berwick and Innes House on his estate near Elgin. Asquith's principal recreation was golf, and when he became Chancellor of the Exchequer in 1905 in Sir Henry Campbell-Bannerman's government, he and his family began to come annually to Glen of Rothes House near Elgin during the shooting season, although they spent most of their time on the links at Lossiemouth. He and his wife were keen golfers and brought their children and their guests to play. Among others, Herbert Gladstone, the chief Liberal Whip, Sir John Dickson-Poynder, M.P., Lady Constance Hatch and Sir John Brodick, Secretary of State for India, frequently played golf with them on the course.

Each year the month of August attracted a full complement of visitors and members to the links at Stotfield. In August of 1913 Herbert Asquith, the Prime Minister since 1908, was enjoying his usual golfing holiday at Lossiemouth whilst staying at Hopeman Lodge with his daughter as guests of G.E. Gordon Duff of Drummuir. For two weeks he had played almost daily over the links and had enjoyed games with Arthur Balfour — soon to serve under him as First Lord of the Admiralty — and Ramsay MacDonald, the leader of the Labour party. On a lovely summer afternoon Asquith and his daughter set off for a round at half past three o'clock and approached the seventeenth green (now the eighteenth green of the New course) two hours later accompanied by their young caddies and two detectives at a discreet distance.

Two well-dressed young ladies had been seen by other golfers sitting beside the green for some time and when Asquith, quite unsuspecting, arrived on the putting surface he was at once set upon. According to a contemporary account he was seized by both arms and subjected to vigorous hustling and tugging at his clothes, his hat was knocked off and one of the suffragists was laying on his head with a magazine. His daughter went to his aid but the detectives and a policeman rescued him. Apparently unperturbed, he and his daughter played the eighteenth hole and he was greeted at the clubhouse by the ringing cheers of the assembled crowd.

The same crowd hissed the women repeatedly and shouts of "duck them in the water" and other less complimentary expressions were heard. The detectives, without loss of time, removed the women to Lossiemouth Police Office, and they were afterwards conveyed to Elgin Police Office by Chief Constable Mair and Detective-Inspector Clarkson of Scotland Yard, in a motor car, the automobile being driven off amidst the hisses of the excited crowd.

They appeared before Sheriff Dunlop in court at Elgin and gave what were thought to be the fictitious names of Winnie Wallace of Dundee, and Flora Helen Smith of Edinburgh. (It is still widely held that one of them was Mrs Pankhurst's daughter, Christabel Pankhurst, Ll.B.). Charged with assault and breach of the peace "they emitted a declaration" and pleaded not guilty. Bail, fixed at £5, was not forthcoming and they were incarcerated in Inverness prison until the money was paid the following day. They returned to Lossiemouth and occasioned a further sensation on the Sunday by attending Duffus Parish Church where the Prime Minister worshipped.

There they seated themselves in the manse pew from which they could obtain an uninterrupted view of Asquith and his daughter, and stared persistently at him throughout the service. After the service they hurried outside and took up a position from which they contented themselves by shouting "hypocrite" at the Prime Minister as he entered his waiting car. The whole incident created a considerable stir in the quiet little village of Duffus.

On the day of their trial in Elgin proceedings were stopped and the case was withdrawn on instructions from Crown Counsel. The young ladies continued to frequent the golf course and were to be seen in the company of a large number of caddies who kept them amused by their quips and jokes, but there was no further disorder. Unlike his friend Ramsay MacDonald, Herbert Asquith was to continue to play golf at Lossiemouth.

From 1906 large numbers of women campaigned for the vote on the streets throughout Britain. Of the three distinct groups of women's suffrage movements the Women's Social and Political Union, founded by Mrs Emmeline Pankhurst, alone adopted militant tactics in the struggle for the vote. The term "suffragette" was coined by the *Daily Mail* to distinguish the militancy of the W.S.P.U. from the constitutional means of the National Union of Women's Suffrage Societies.

Militant suffragettes were very active in 1913. The tea pavilion in Kew Gardens in London was burned to the ground in February, the Old Manchester golf club pavilion was set on fire, and corrosive liquid was thrown about the Horsforth golf links near Leeds. In April they burned down a stand at Ayr racecourse, but the most dramatic episode of all occurred on Derby day, June 5th, when Miss Emily Davison flung herself under King George V's horse Anmer at Epsom's Tattenham Corner and died of a fractured skull. Four days later two suffragettes set fire to the main stand at Hurst Park racecourse and caused thousands of pounds worth of damage. The Prime Minister and the Moray Golf Club may well have been fortunate.

The Warning-off of Ramsay MacDonald

This strange story, until now engrossed in copperplate handwriting in a volume of the minutes of the Moray Golf Club, has been well known to many past captains who have read it with interest and not a little surprise. What happened to Ramsay MacDonald at the hands of the members of the Moray Golf Club is frequently recounted in Moray, and much further afield, and the facts are as frequently misrepresented.

In August of 1915 James Ramsay MacDonald, Lossie "loon" and Member of Parliament for Leicester since 1906, had been a member of the golf club from its earliest years in the 1890's and was an enthusiastic if not a distinguished golfer, much like any other member. He was a keen walker, and played golf almost daily when at his Lossiemouth home. But his days at 10, Downing Street as the first Labour Prime Minister had not yet arrived and his views on the war were completely at variance with the temper of the times and with that of his own party.

Ramsay MacDonald at the starter's box with Alister and Malcolm — 1909

This led to his resignation as leader of the Labour party soon after the outbreak of war and the appointment of Arthur Henderson as the new leader. As a prominent member of the Labour party, and as a pacifist Ramsay MacDonald was not acceptable to some members of the Moray Golf Club. His outspoken opposition to the war was characteristic of the man who, from his earliest days of poverty, displayed that moral (and physical) courage which later endeared him to an army of admirers and even gained the respect of his bitterest opponents. Long after his death at sea in 1937 many bitter opponents with long memories remained — and remain to this day — in the Labour party.

29

The first "Requisition", claiming that the character and interests of the golf club were being endangered by him remaining a member, was read to the Council at its meeting of 19th August 1915. It was signed by twenty members, the first signature being that of John Foster, Sheriff Clerk of Morayshire and captain of the golf club. Other signatories were Lewis Noad of London, John F. Cumming of Aberlour on Speyside, H.C. Willock-Pollen, Lord of the Manor of Little Bookham in Surrey, Canon Hay-Dinwoodie of Elgin, A. Grigor Jeans and Ronald Jeans of Liverpool and Dr C. A. Trouncer of Surrey who had been a member for three months.

The Council decided to call a special general meeting and the secretary was instructed to write to Ramsay MacDonald in terms of rule 26, to send him the requisition, and ask him to submit a statement or explanation.

Ramsay MacDonald had friends of all political persuasions who kept him abreast of developments in the golf club. J. Hay Glennie, Elgin lawyer and Town Clerk of Lossiemouth, wrote on the night of the Council meeting.

Seaview,
Lossiemouth
19 Aug 1915

My dear MacDonald,

I have just come in from the Golf Club House where I have been contending that we have nothing whatever to do with your political utterances. The Captain [Foster] and some others were present. I don't know that I have done any good but I believe I have done no harm. I am rather inclined to think this movement, if it did not originate on personal grounds, has now developed on that footing, and this I need not say I deprecate.

From the rumours I hear I doubt if a motion to expel you would carry, but what troubles me is how I should vote. I certainly would vote against such a motion if I were sure that capital would not be made of a defeated motion in Germany. I hope you will understand the fix I would be in. Now I am told tonight that you have been given an opportunity to "lie low" here during the war. I sincerely hope you will avail yourself of this chance, not to save your own "neck" (pardon the expression), but for the sake of your friends. If you accept this note in the spirit in which it is written you will not consider it impertinence.

Yours very sincerely,

J.H. Glennie.

P.S. [Ernest] Humbert called on me on Sunday night, good chap! He was very bellicose but I advised him to find a *via media*. I meet McIsaac [Elgin lawyer and Council member] at lunch daily. Yesterday he was in a highly "patriotic" mood and was for expulsion and so was his son — who by the way should be at the front — but today he (James!) was more amiable and told me he had written to the Secretary suggesting a way out of the difficulty which he hoped would be adopted.

I had contended with McIsaac that you were to a large extent misrepresented and told him that Macdonald (Drainie) had told me that Jeans [Liverpool newspaper magnate] was relenting. McIsaac told me today that he had called on MacDonald last night.

At the next meeting the secretary read a letter from J. M. Fraser, an Elgin banker, expressing surprise that the requisition, with the names of those who had signed it, had appeared in the press. The secretary stated that it had not come from his office and he then read Ramsay MacDonald's reply.

The Hillocks,
Lossiemouth
24th August 1915.

Sir,

Moray Golf Club

I am in receipt of your letter of 20th inst. enclosing a copy of a Requisition and asking if I have any observations to make upon it. I have two points to comment upon.

I did not join the Moray Golf Club because of my views upon politics. There is nothing in the Constitution or purpose of the club which imposes an obligation upon its members to form political opinions and utter political criticisms only in accordance with the tastes of those who signed this Requisition or of any other section of persons who happen to be members of the club.

If either the Council or a General Meeting of members propose to alter the Constitution of the club and the qualification for membership in the direction indicated above, I hope they will do so in such a definite way as will protect those who may propose to join the club in future from such personal insult as that offered to me by this Requisition and its signatories.

My second point relates to the Council itself, the action of which is not clear from your letter, and about which I must ask you to be good enough to give me some further explanation.

The method of expulsion is dealt with in rule 26 and in consequence, cannot be dealt with as ordinary club business under rule 7. In rule 26 the procedure is laid down in terms that are quite specific. Before any resolution for the expulsion of a member can come before a meeting of the club, the Council must by a two-thirds majority of its members (not even of those present but of the total of its members) suspend the member in question.

Only for one or two purposes can the Council order such a letter as you have written to be addressed to any member of the club. You may address me before my suspension asking for any explanation, or after my suspension, and only seven days before the meeting, asking if I am willing to withdraw.

Your letter is neither one thing nor the other though you say it is written in accordance with rule 26. Under this rule both the Requisition and the decision of the Council to call a Special Meeting of members are irregular.

Yours faithfully,
(sgd) J. Ramsay MacDonald

A. F. MacDonald Esq.,
Secy., Moray Golf Club.

One can but conjecture whether or not he had taken legal advice. It is clear that he had read Rule 26 closely, and that his carefully argued letter was a correct interpretation of it. It seems unlikely that his keen mind required any assistance, and at this stage he was certainly more than a match for the Council of the Moray Golf Club. Lewis Noad had as yet played a comparatively minor role.

Rule XXVI. — Expulsion

If the conduct of any Member is such as appears to the Council to endanger the character, interests, or good order of the Club, or if any Member shall wilfully disobey any order of the Council communicated to him, it shall be in the power of the Council, after calling upon the Member for an explanation, to suspend such Member on a vote of two-thirds of its number. The Club shall have power at any Meeting to pass a resolution to remove the name of such Member from the Roll of Members, if, in the opinion of two-thirds of those voting (which shall be by ballot), he has, by his conduct, forfeited his right to remain a Member, provided notice of such resolution be placed on the card of business of such Meeting. Seven days before calling such Meeting the Council shall communicate with the offending Member to give him an opportunity of withdrawing from the Club.

The following day he wrote to a friend.

The Hillocks,
Lossiemouth.
25th August 1915.

.......They are trying to expel me from the Golf Club here and that is worrying.
The place is infested by snobs and "penny gentry" in the summer. They may succeed.
I would not mind very much if it were not for [my sons] Alister and Malcolm who are
also members and who of course feel it without fully understanding it.

Some of my swell Tory friends are rallying round me splendidly. The old dowager
Countess and her daughter are coming up next week just to show me countenance,
and an aristocratic candidate (Tory) for a Scottish county wants to come and play golf
with me for two days and cut everybody else...........

Horatio Bottomley attempted to dishonour him by publishing his birth
certificate in *John Bull*, in September 1915, showing he was illegitimate,
and that his mother had registered his name as James MacDonald Ramsay.
John Bull went so far as to state that MacDonald should be tried as a traitor
and shot because of his anti-war campaign. H.G. Wells, the socialist
intellectual, described MacDonald and his friends as "the shabbiest scum
of socialism".

Few people were aware that MacDonald had himself been to the front.
According to Lord Elton "in December 1914 he arrived in Belgium with
an ambulance unit organised by Dr Hector Munro. The following day he
had disappeared and agitated enquiry disclosed that he had been arrested
and sent back to Britain. At home he saw Lord Kitchener who expressed
his annoyance at the incident and gave instructions for him to be given
an "omnibus" pass to the whole of the Western Front.

"He returned to an entirely different reception and was met by General
Seeley at Poperinghe who expressed his regrets at the way MacDonald
had been treated. They set off for the front at Ypres and soon found
themselves in the thick of an action in which both behaved with the utmost
coolness. Later, MacDonald was received by the Commander-in-Chief at
St Omer and made an extensive tour of the front.

"Returning home, he paid a public tribute to the courage of the French
troops, but said nothing then or later of having been under fire himself."
This was a side of which the public and
the members of the Moray Golf Club
were to remain entirely unaware.

Some Council members had not
been idle since the receipt of
MacDonald's letter. James McIsaac had
put in writing that the provisions of rule
26 should be complied with and the
resolution to call the Special Meeting
rescinded. The captain, John Foster,
moved that the Council deal with the
requisition under Rule 7, but this was
heavily defeated by a proposal that the
procedure should be under Rule 26.
Standing Orders were suspended and
the resolution calling a special general
meeting was overturned after another
vote.

James McIsaac

Rule VII. — Special Meetings.

Special Meetings of the Club may be called by the Council, or on a requisition to the Secretary signed by not less than ten Members. Such Meeting shall be called by circular, giving not less than seven days' notice thereof, and stating the business to be considered.

The secretary was instructed to write MacDonald and ask for an explanation with regard to the requisition. The Council met to consider his reply.

The Hillocks, Lossiemouth,
2nd September 1915

Dear Sir, **Moray Golf Club.**

I am in receipt of yours of the 31st ulto. informing me that the Council has reconsidered the decision of its previous meeting and rescinded it, and intimating that it now proposes "to proceed with the matter raised in the Requisition under Rule 26 of the Constitution". To enable it to do this, you request me to give you an explanation regarding the Requisition.

The Council, however, must first of all state to me definitely what it objects to, and must take upon itself the responsibility of making charges against my conduct as a Member of the Club or as affecting my membership of the Club. That is clearly laid down in Rule 26.

Of the Requisition itself it has neither order nor decency to commend it. It complies with no provision of the Constitution. It is nothing but a political document, signed by political partisans and animated by a variety of political animosities — most of them of very long standing vigour. I can therefore only refer you to what I wrote in the opening sentences of my last letter on the subject.

If the Council in the exercise of its duties as the custodian of the interests of a golf club should address to me any complaint that specifically states what is complained of, I shall always do my best to assist the Council in its work and comply with its requests.

Yours faithfully,
(Sgd.) J. Ramsay MacDonald.

This put the cat among the pigeons, and the Council began to waver. The idea that MacDonald might have taken legal advice and the thought that they might land the Moray Golf Club in the soup would have greatly exercised the members of the Council. The Council of management of the golf club consisted of the captain and vice-captain and nine Councillors, of whom four were resident in Lossiemouth and seven in Elgin.

Alexander Grant of McVitie & Price had written to MacDonald from London on 1st September 1915.

......I was greatly distressed to see by Saturday's Elgin paper what has been going on in Lossie about the Golf Club and, if there is to be a meeting, I am going North to it, however busy I may be. I really feel sorry for those people knowing how much they will regret it afterwards, as I consider it one of the most childish and meanest things I have heard of for a long time......

John Foster was much more determined than his fellow Council members and he proposed that Ramsay MacDonald be suspended there and then. McIsaac moved as an amendment:

That with reference to the letter from Mr Ramsay MacDonald of 2nd inst., the Secretary is instructed to state in reply that there is prevalent a very strong feeling that the matter involved is not one of politics but of patriotism, and that his reported utterances in connection with the War have been quoted with approval and disseminated by the German Press as those of one who has charged Sir Edward Grey with having deceived his countrymen and who holds that Germany was attacked and was not the aggressor.

The Council express their strong disapproval of Mr Ramsay MacDonald's reported utterances, but consider it unnecessary at present that any further steps should be taken in the matter. The Secretary is instructed to communicate to each of the Requisitionists the foregoing finding of the Council, but (beyond replying to Mr Ramsay MacDonald's letter) not to make any communication to him without further instructions.

McIsaac's amendment was successful by five votes to three. John Hunter, the vice-captain, declined to vote on the ground that the issue was entirely political. The first paragraph of the amendment was duly despatched as a letter to Ramsay MacDonald on 10th September 1915. MacDonald had written to R.I. Cameron before he received the letter.

R.I. Cameron

London.
September 11th 1915.

My dear Cameron,

I see in the London papers yesterday and today that the Council of the Club has declined to suspend me. I assume by that that they have again had to follow my constitutional advice and accept my challenge to put Rule 26 into operation in a proper way, with the result as published. I think three members of the Council signed the requisition; were they the same three who voted for suspension?

I have got back to London from Bristol and am now settling down for several weeks. I had a very fine time at the Trade Union Congress. I don't know what your northern papers have reported but I had a far better reception, both when I rose to speak and when I sat down, than Lloyd George had, so you see you must not be led too much by newspaper criticism.

I hear from the children that they tried to get yours to go to Covesea last week but failed. They were very sad. You seem to have excellent weather and I wish I were back. We have had a narrow squeak here with the Zeppelins. Six people were killed in a house not far from here.

With kindest regards to Mrs Cameron and yourself.

I am,
Yours very sincerely,
J. Ramsay MacDonald.

Cameron replied.

Elgin.
13th September 1915.

My dear MacDonald,

I have yours of the 11th inst., and am delighted you got such a good reception at Bristol; you were well reported in all the Scotch papers, and I liked every word of your speech.

In the Moray Golf Club Council, the three members who voted for your suspension were the three members of the Council who signed the requisition — Foster (captain), Lawson and Cormack. They tried to make proceedings in the Council strictly private, and appealed to the other members to let nothing go out to the Press, but I motored down to Lossiemouth in the evening, got all details, returned to Elgin, and wired to all the Scotch papers including some London ones; they are now trying to find me out. You'll get a letter from them about you being unpatriotic etc., and you will now know how to answer them.

I expect I will be back in London soon, as it looks as if McKenna [Chancellor of the Exchequer] were going to have a try to increase the spirit duty, but I have no doubt the Irish will give to him what they gave to George. I am convinced that any increase in the spirit duty would lead to a decrease in the revenue, and be a contentious measure. You might let me know by wire or otherwise as soon as anything definite is decided upon.

I hear your family and mine are to be at some ploy tomorrow.

With kind regards,
I am,
Yours very sincerely,
R.I. Cameron.

At the next meeting on 16th October the secretary read a letter from Sir Roderick Wigan, Bt., of Surrey, intimating his own and Lady Wigan's resignations as they could not remain members as long as Ramsay MacDonald was a member, and H.V. Masefield requested that his own and his wife's name be removed from the list for the same reason. (Sir Roderick's father-in-law, Lewis D. Wigan of Glenalmond in Perthshire, was to be one of the signatories of the second petition against MacDonald.) As there were only three Council members present the secretary was instructed to bring up the letters at the next meeting.

The next meeting was also poorly attended and a letter from Ramsay MacDonald was read and allowed to "lie on the table". This letter was not engrossed in the minutes but it undoubtedly caused more discomfiture for a now very uncertain committee.

September 16th 1915.

Dear Sir,

I have received your letter of the 10th inst., but really I do not know what it means or what is its purpose.

On Friday afternoon on my return from Bristol I noticed in the evening papers a specially displayed paragraph stating that your Council, by five votes to three, had declined to suspend me, and some of them had rather sarcastic remarks about the Moray Golf Club for ever taking any action at all. In your letter you make no mention of this but simply inform me that in the Council's view (though even that is not clear) "the matter involved is not one of politics but one of patriotism". I hope the Council will not consider me offensive if I say that neither with regard to politics nor to patriotism do I place the least value on its opinion. Even were I responsible for the grotesque things which the German press has published or the malicious lies and perversions which partisan newspapers in this country have circulated, the Council of a golf club is not the authority to pronounce judgment either upon what I as a politician have said or what I am **said** to have said. It has been elected to perform such duties as to reprimand members for taking dogs on to the course, to preserve sobriety in the clubhouse, to see that gentlemen do not insult ladies — and Radicals — on the course, and to put appropriate penalties on rabbit scrapes, ditches and persons who play too well.

Your letter, however, is so mysterious in view of the newspaper paragraphs to which I have referred, and to your previous statement that the Council was about to proceed under Rule XXVI that I can only assume you must have made some mistake about it.

Yours truly,

(Sgd.) J. Ramsay MacDonald.

The Twenty-eighth annual general meeting of the Moray Golf Club was held within the Burgh Court House, Elgin, on 2nd March 1916. After the usual business, a discussion took place in secret session about the requisition in regard to Ramsay MacDonald and whether the Council were justified in not calling a special meeting of the club. MacDonald was kept informed.

Southview,
Elgin
10/3/1916

My dear MacDonald,

Yesterday on receipt of your letter I sent for Watt [the editor of] The Courant. He has reproduced it in today's Courant. Your letters were all read at the [annual] meeting and Foster, Lawson and Cormack were speechless. They made no answer. McIsaac spoke for twenty minutes and condemned the Requisition in strong language. Wilken [Aberdeen Free Press] and Watt think your victory complete.

Yours sincerely,

R.I. Cameron

These two shrewd newspapermen had not understood the lengths to which Foster and his friends were prepared to go. The minutes, normally so detailed, now become curiously vague. At a meeting of the new Council on 13th March 1916 the minutes record:— "Mr Foster referred to the paragraph which appeared in last Friday's *Elgin Courant.* The Council records its regret that a member who was present at the Annual Meeting, which conducted its business in private, should have been guilty of such a breach of faith as to communicate such business to the Press. The communication is not in accordance with the facts."

The report in *The Courant* contained extracts from an anonymous letter from a member of the club and read:

> Great publicity was given during the past summer to the action of a very small section of the members of the Moray Golf Club who attempted to expel Mr Ramsay MacDonald, M.P., from the club, but, as the meetings were always held in private, the public were never actually informed as to the result of the requisition. At the annual meeting of the club last week, Mr David West again brought up the subject, and asked that [all] the correspondence on the subject be read, but the secretary had hardly made a commencement when the captain moved that the meeting be held in private.
>
> Mr West appeared to be in favour of the matter being dealt with in public, and he thought the press should be supplied with a paragraph. The minutes read at the recent meeting showed that out of eleven members of the Council, only three members favoured suspension and these three signed a requisition which had to come before themselves for judgment. At the recent meeting a member pointed out that rule 26 made clear that there must be two-thirds of a majority [on the Council] before any member can be suspended and seven members of the Council must vote for suspension. The finding, therefore, is that Mr MacDonald remains a member of the Moray Golf Club.

The Second Petition

In the next few months a new Representation against MacDonald began to circulate. It appeared in its final form with thirty signatures appended — but eleven of the twenty who signed the first one had retired from the fray, including John Cormack, Canon Hay-Dinwoodie, J.M. Fraser, John F. Cumming of Aberlour, George G. Anderson of The Oriental Club, London, and Dr Trouncer of Surrey. At the annual general meeting three members of the Council had retired, and J.B. Mair, Angus Macdonald and John Gibbon were elected in their places. Angus Macdonald was the sole Council signatory of the second petition.

What was to follow showed a distinct meanness of spirit allied to a simple desire to wound — perhaps a reaction engendered by the times. Conscription of all males from eighteen to forty-one years of age had been introduced early in 1916 and the battle of the Somme had opened on July 1st 1916. The papers were daily full of huge casualty lists, some 60,000 casualties on the first day of the battle alone, and some apologists might think it not too difficult to understand the anger and resentment which became focused on this particular member of a golf club.

The Council met on 7th August 1916 and the captain, John Foster, Sheriff Clerk of Morayshire, introduced the following resolution.

> Having considered the Representation dated 1st August 1916 signed by thirty members regarding the membership of Mr Ramsay MacDonald M.P., the Secretary is instructed (after having given Mr MacDonald seven days notice) to call a Special General Meeting for the first day of September 1916 within the Burgh Court House, Elgin at 6 p.m. at which the following resolution will be submitted :— That this Special General Meeting of the Club is of the opinion that Mr Ramsay MacDonald's public utterances regarding the war have led to resignations from the club and to grave dissatisfaction among its members; confirms the finding of the Council that his conduct

is such as to endanger the character and interests of the Club; declares that he has forfeited his right to remain a member, and resolves that his name be removed from the roll.

To his lasting credit the vice-captain, John Hunter, the Lossiemouth schoolmaster, moved an amendment at this meeting "that no steps be taken, as Mr Ramsay MacDonald's conduct has not been such as to endanger the character or interests of the Club, and that the motion is against the Constitution of the Club". He failed to find a seconder and Cameron wrote to MacDonald.

Southview, Elgin.
11/8/16

My dear MacDonald,

It was only on Saturday last I heard Foster was moving against you. He got 30 signatures to the petition this time. All of them bitter political enemies of yours. The Council is also changed as you know, and changed in his favour but not yet unanimous about putting it to the vote of a general meeting of the members. I do not think he has ever got the required two thirds majority in this Council but he must be very near it this time. We will fight him up to the end. To get a two thirds majority at a general meeting is a large order for him to carry. Do not think of resignation or anything else. Malcolm and Ishbel are old enough to laugh at the attempt. Keep your legal friend watching their moves. I think they are very near legal proceedings. The Council must act in accordance with their Rules. McIsaac warned them well at the last Annual Meeting the risks they were running of a legal action. I will write whenever I hear anything.

Yours sincerely,
R.I.Cameron.

The Representation from the thirty members read as follows:

We desire to represent to the Council that the question of Mr Ramsay MacDonald's membership, which was left unsettled by the last Council, is the cause of much dissatisfaction to many members who are concerned to learn that there have been resignations from the Club consequent upon his remaining a member and who are apprehensive that the same cause may lead to more resignations and may prevent other people from joining the Club. The situation is obviously injurious to the Club's welfare. We trust the Council may take an early opportunity of considering this requisition and we see no reason why it should not be dealt with now and in accordance with the Club's constitution.

The question is far beyond ordinary political differences. The last Council recognised this and minuted that the matter "was not one of politics but of patriotism" and that MacDonald's conduct appeared to them "to endanger the character and interests of the Club". We complain that his public utterances regarding the war are of such a nature as to render his membership objectionable and that they have led directly to resignations.

We select the following specific instances which require no comment. In the *Labour Leader* he wrote "When Sir Edward Grey failed to secure peace between Germany and Russia he worked deliberately to involve us in the war using Belgium as his chief excuse" and again "his shortsightedness and his blunders have brought all this upon us". In *The Pioneer* of 17th August 1914, he wrote "there is no doubt whatever that when all is over and we turn back to it (Sir Edward Grey's speech) in cold blood and read it carefully, so as to ascertain why England has practically declared war on Germany, we shall find that the only reason from beginning to end in it is that our Foreign Office is anti-German and that the Admiralty was anxious to seize any opportunity of using the Navy in battle practice".

In *The Leicester Pioneer* of August 7th 1914, he wrote that "never did we arm our people and ask them to give us their lives for less good cause than this". In the light of what is happening today it is interesting to recall Mr MacDonald's diagnosis in August 1908 — "It is the fathers and — alas that one should say it — the mothers of these coddled officers who, in spite of their privileges, could not produce one per cent of

37

decent fighting men who are the enemy. It is people who want titles who are telling you today that Germany is arming to blow up London with a fleet of airships."

These and other utterances have been used by the German Press to slander our country and have actually been circulated in Britain by German Agencies. In a letter to the *Berliner Tageblatt,* headed "Brave Men" occurs the sentence— "Now he (Mr Ramsay MacDonald) has attacked Grey in Parliament in the course of a violent speech, accusing him of having knowingly and deliberately deceived his country ", and Krupps organ the *Rheinische Westfaelische Zeitung,* referring to one of his articles, stated that "This is another sign that the bitter truth is beginning to dawn on England."

Further, letters were sent enclosing copies of Mr MacDonald's speeches to the relatives of British soldiers who were killed in defending him and us. It is true that he disclaims responsibility for the circulation of these, but he does not and cannot deny that he provided the material for them. We regard their author's attempts at explanation as paltry and disingenuous, showing, as has been said, "but an uneasy conviction of having miscalculated the chances". We and many other members resent his association with the Club and believe his membership to be contrary to its interests and welfare.

We respectfully suggest to the Council that the matter should now be dealt with in accordance with the Constitution of the Club and ask them to take proceedings under Rule 26, or as they may decide, in order to get the considered verdict of the Club at a General Meeting on the question whether the offending member's name should be removed from the roll.

The groundwork had been thoroughly laid and the outcome of the special general meeting was never in doubt. The charged atmosphere in which the proceedings were held was heightened by the resignations from the Council of vice-captain John Hunter and past-captain J.B. Mair, M.V.O., Chief Constable of Elgin, which were announced at a Council meeting in the secretary's office in Elgin on the very day of the special meeting. This Council meeting was ostensibly held to deal with the preliminaries to the special meeting — except for one strange circumstance. Eight new members were admitted to the club at the meeting, and four of them — T.A. Simpson of Banff, Sydney Stewart of the North of Scotland Bank, Elgin, F. Davis, Central Bar, Elgin, and Thomas B.Mather, Masonic Bar, Lossiemouth — were present and voting at the special meeting a few hours later. On 22nd July, T.A. Simpson and his wife had played at Lossiemouth as guests of John Foster, the captain.

Ninety-eight members gathered in the Burgh Court House of Elgin — an appropriate setting — on the evening of Friday 1st day of September 1916. John Foster was in the chair and was immediately challenged by R.I. Cameron who suggested, in view of Foster's identification with the Representation, that a neutral chairman be appointed. This did not find favour and Foster remained in the chair.

Letters of apology were read from John H. Perry, London, W.J. Capes, Glasgow, J.B. Taylor, Dundee, Lord Algernon Gordon Lennox, London, Captain Mair, British Expeditionary Force, France, E.M. Hutchinson, Liverpool, and A.G. Jeans also of Liverpool.

The chairman stated that statements had been received from three members, Dr John S. Fairbairn, London, Dr Edgar Collis, London, and A.G. Jeans, Liverpool, and asked if these should be read. After a motion from the floor that the meeting proceed to the business on the card, Lewis Noad proposed that all the statements should be read and this was seconded by Alexander Grant. The captain read Dr Fairbairn's statement. After hearing it the meeting declined to have any further statements read on behalf of either side.

Dr Fairbairn's statement.

42. Wimpole Street,
London, W.
August 26, 1916.

....my opposition to this motion is entirely on the question of principle and has nothing to do with the views expressed by Mr Ramsay MacDonald, any sympathy with which I entirely repudiate. ....I take it that this meeting must be convinced that the limit of free expression of political views has been exceeded, before the public conduct of a member of a club devoted to sport and recreation can be called in question by his fellow-members.

....The bare statement of the Council that this is a question of patriotism and not of politics merely begs the question. The members of the Council were selected for their wisdom in golfing matters and not as authorities on political science. The signatories to the representation have stepped in where the angels of the Council feared to tread, and have tried to justify themselves by quotations from the member's writings, which date from the very beginning of the war, when stronger heads than his had lost their bearings....

....He held in 1908, and continued to hold in 1914, an ideal of what is right and proper for the country differing absolutely from that of the vast majority of us, but if he consistently and conscientiously holds and expresses such ideas, on what ground do the members of his golf club brand them as unpatriotic? Surely not simply because they don't like them. Again, if such views were expressed in 1908, and were unpatriotic then, why has the club waited eight years to rid itself of this turbulent fellow? It looks as if the war had affected the nerves of its members.

....The signatories say his utterances have been of use to the Germans. We know that the Huns will use anything they think will serve their purpose, but this very use of their opinions by the Germans has been entirely repudiated by the press and by public men as a test of unpatriotic action, on the ground that it is equivalent to checking all criticism of the Government and powers that be — a cherished British privilege which has been exercised to the full throughout the war.

One terrible utterance they quote, made against Sir Edward Grey, as he then was, "his shortsightedness and his blunders have brought all this upon us", is nothing to what *The Times* and other papers said about his diplomacy in the Balkans and his conduct of the blockade, and still stronger words have been used against other Ministers of the Crown, from the Prime Minister downwards, all of which have been gloated over by the German press, and have given so much the greater joy to the Huns as coming from more influential quarters. Let me remind you of the Northcliffe attacks on the late Lord Kitchener, which led to the childish but harmless episode of the burning of one of his papers on the London Stock Exchange.

I have heard of golf clubs from which it was proposed to exclude the Northcliffe papers, but I have yet to learn of the club from which a member has been expelled for speaking harsh words against a Minister of the Crown, even if his words have been favourably received in Germany, and I trust that the Moray Golf Club may not earn this unenviable distinction....

There is no accusation against the prisoner at the bar of disturbing the amenities of the club. Doubtless the signatories would overlook intemperance in other ways, even in the clubhouse itself, but intemperance in political speeches made hundred of miles away is too much for the nerves. They unearth writings from papers no one has ever heard of, like the *Leicester Pioneer* and the *Labour Leader,* and having given them a publicity they did not deserve, they frighten the life out of the docile Council by talking of resignations, and expect us to believe that anyone who wished to, and could come to Lossiemouth, would be deterred by this new bogey of the course from playing on it....

The agitation is mean and petty, because it is just one of those things best left alone. Hunting a heretic only produces a sympathy for the victim and a more lenient view of his heresies. It is the opening of contentious matters of this kind that endanger the character and interests of the club.

Yours, etc.,   John S. Fairbairn.

The Secretary stated that Dr Fairbairn
had also requested that it be recorded in
the Minute that he protested against the
motion. The Chairman ruled it out of
order to record any such protest.

Mr Lewis Noad then moved :

"That this Special General Meeting of
the Club is of opinion that Mr.
Ramsay Macdonald's public utter
:ances regarding the War have led
to resignations from the Club and
to grave dissatisfaction among its
members : confirms the finding
of the Council that his conduct
is such as to endanger the
character and interests of the
Club ; declares that he has for:
:feited his right to remain a
Member and resolves that his name
be removed from the roll"

The motion was seconded by Mr. S.
McCall Smith.

Mr Hunter, Mr Cameron and Mr
Sutherland spoke in opposition to the
motion

After Mr Noad had replied the vote was
taken by ballot.

On the voting papers being counted
there were found to be in favour of the motion
73 votes and against the motion 24 votes

As the requisite majority of two-thirds
of those voting had been obtained in
favour of the motion the Chairman de:
:clared the same to be carried

The /.

The Motion to expel Ramsay MacDonald — 1st September 1916

Lewis Noad then moved "That this Special General Meeting of the Club is of opinion that Mr Ramsay MacDonald's public utterances regarding the War have led to resignations from the Club and to grave dissatisfaction among its members: confirms the findings of the Council that his conduct is such as to endanger the character and interests of the Club: declares that he has forfeited his right to remain a Member and resolves that his name be removed from the roll." The motion was seconded by S. McCall Smith.

John Hunter, R. Innes Cameron and John E. Sutherland, M.P. for Morayshire, spoke in opposition to the motion. After Lewis Noad had replied the vote was taken by ballot. In favour of the motion there were 73 votes and against the motion 24 votes. As the requisite majority of two-thirds of those voting had been obtained the chairman declared it carried and the meeting ended.

These are the words of the minutes and only a little more can be gleaned from the local newspapers of the day. *The Elgin Courant and Courier* in its edition of 8th September states that no official report of the proceedings was supplied.

> They were informed, however, that the question of appointing a neutral chairman was raised by Mr R. Innes Cameron, who said that as Mr Foster had identified himself with these petitions in such a way that they had come to be known as "The Foster Petitions", a neutral chairman should be appointed.
>
> Letters were read both in favour of and against the petition. Dr Fairbairn, of 42, Wimpole Street, London, wrote strongly against the petition being considered at all, while Mr Jeans and Mr Hutchinson of Liverpool, wrote strongly in favour of the petition. (The minute states that Dr Fairbairn's letter was the only one read to the meeting).
>
> The adoption of the Council's resolution was moved by a London barrister, Mr Lewis Noad, who dealt exclusively with Mr MacDonald as a politician and discussed his public utterances on the war. The speech is described as being an exceedingly able one, wholly free from personalities, and marked by calm, moderate, and clear reasoning. Mr John Hunter, Lossiemouth, vice-captain of the club, who has now resigned from that office, gave his reasons for so doing and spoke against the motion.
>
> Mr R. Innes Cameron raised the question of the irregularity of the proceedings. He held that, under rule 26, there must be a majority of eight in the Council before there could be suspension and it was admitted that there was only a majority of six. In consequence of this any conclusion arrived at could not be carried out. If the procedure was regular, he asked why a general meeting was not called a year ago when the first petition came before the Council.
>
> Mr John E. Sutherland, M.P., — member of Parliament for the Elgin Burghs — spoke against the petition. He made it clear that he had no sympathy of any kind with Mr MacDonald's views, but he held that as a golf club they had nothing to do with Mr MacDonald as a politician. On no account should the golf club turn itself into a political club. He instanced the case of Lord Morley, who resigned his seat in the Cabinet on account of his views on the war, and was still a power for good in the House of Lords.

The national newspapers carried short reports of the expulsion and a good deal of hostile comment on the club's action appeared in the local newspapers, but there was no reaction from Ramsay MacDonald until *The Elgin Courant* published the following letters on 6th October.

9, Howitt Road, Hampstead, N.W.

To The Editor.

Dear Sir,

Mr Ramsay MacDonald desires me to send you the enclosed letter, which at the same time, is going to the Press.

Yours faithfully,

V. A. Reed, Private Secretary

A. F. MacDonald, Esq.,
Hon. Secretary of the Moray Golf Club.

Sir,

I am in receipt of your letter informing me that the Moray Golf Club has decided to become a political association with a golf course attached, and that, regarding my own membership, it has torn up its rules in order that some of its members may give rein to their political prejudice and spite.

Unfortunately, for some years, the visit of any prominent Liberal or Radical to the Moray Golf Club has been resented by a certain section which has not concealed its offensiveness either in the Club House or on the course.

Though I am, therefore, not sorry that the character of a number of members of the Moray Golf Club has been advertised to the world, I cannot help regretting that the Club, of which I am one of the earliest members, should be held up to public ridicule and contempt by the childish resolve of these members to annoy those who have far greater claims than they have to the peaceful enjoyment of a holiday at Lossiemouth.

I shall continue to enjoy the delights of Lossiemouth and the friendship of those with whom I care to associate there, irrespective of some of the gentry of Elgin and its neighbourhood and of a certain type of casual strangers who find it convenient to join the Golf Club.

Yours faithfully,
(signed) J. Ramsay MacDonald.

Rarely can a political episode have been so carefully chronicled in the minutes of a golf club. Perhaps it was for posterity or, much more likely, in anticipation of a possible legal action. Looking back on this extraordinary affair over seventy years later when all the protagonists are dead, the author is struck by the fact that although he played golf with a number of those close to the events, including one of the signatories to the second petition, he cannot recall that it ever came up in the course of conversation. Nor had he the good sense ever to ask Mrs Ishbel Peterkin (Ramsay MacDonald's daughter) about it, although she was a friend for many years. She was to become a member of the golf club in 1921 from her father's address in Hampstead, which suggests that the future Prime Minister was unwilling to allow the antics or eccentricities of his local golf club's members to interfere with his family's pleasure in golf. He had been made an honorary member of Spey Bay golf club some twelve miles to the east and was never to play golf at Lossiemouth again.

Ishbel, Malcolm and Ramsay MacDonald at Spey Bay

42

Ramsay MacDonald's surviving daughters, Mrs Joan MacKinnon and Mrs Sheila Lochhead, have confirmed to the author that this whole episode was a very severe blow to their father who took such delight in returning to his native Lossiemouth. The house in Moray Street named "The Hillocks" was originally built by him for his mother before it became his own home, and is still owned by the family. He had consulted the Lord Advocate about obtaining a court injunction to prevent the special meeting but was advised against it.

The Hillocks

David Marquand in his book *Ramsay MacDonald* writes "Nevertheless, he still seems to have considered going to law — a course from which he was deterred, partly by friends who wisely pointed out that he would be foolish to show publicly how deeply he cared about the whole matter, and partly by the Glasgow pacifist solicitor Rosslyn Mitchell who advised him that although an English court in similar circumstances would be concerned to do equity, a Scottish court would only be concerned to ensure that the formalities had been complied with."

The term "equity" is well known to golfers and can best be defined as fairness or fair play. In *The Rules of Golf,* under Section 3.1(4) it states: "If any point in dispute is not covered by the Rules, the decision shall be made in accordance with equity."

MacDonald had written to Cameron in Elgin to explain the legal niceties.

My dear Cameron,   October 4th 1916.

When I got into my piles of papers that had accumulated when I was in Scotland, I found Munro's [Lord Advocate] letter which I send to you as you would no doubt like to see it in its full extent. You might let me have it back. I discussed the matter with Rosslyn Mitchell when I was staying with him this week-end in Glasgow and he explains the diversity between the opinion of Simon [Home Secretary] and Munro in this way: the practice of the English Courts in a case like this is to do equity; the Scotch practice, however, is simply to see that the formalities are properly complied with.

Mitchell's view is that I could get a decision in the Court of King's Bench but not in the Court of Session and that I would have very little chance unless I was prepared to take it right through to the House of Lords. There, however, I shall drop it. Let me know in due course about the majority required for rescinding. I had not the rules with me when I was in Glasgow but Mitchell is of opinion that a majority of one is sufficient. I will see Simon, however, when the House of Commons meets.

I had a tremendous time in Glasgow. Five thousand people were packed in the St Andrews Hall and nearly as many were kept outside.

With kindest regards,

Yours very sincerely,

J. Ramsay MacDonald.

43

The principal participants in the affair included many notable local personalities and others from much farther afield. Alexander Grant, himself a staunch Conservative, was undoubtedly there to defend his boyhood companion and fellow Morayshire "loon". They had known one another since MacDonald's uncle and Grant's father had both worked together on the old Morayshire railway. Grant will best be remembered for his portrayal on television as the biscuit magnate who, waiting at 10 Downing Street to greet his friend Ramsay MacDonald returning from the House of Commons, is astounded to hear that the Prime Minister commonly travelled about London on the Underground as no official car went with the post. It seems impossible now, but a distinguished political correspondent who had Lossiemouth connections, the late James Margach, relates how "when really pressed for time he [MacDonald] stood on the corner of Downing Street to hail one of the old taxi-cabs".

The impetuous and ever generous Grant at once offers to provide a car and overrides protests that MacDonald could not afford to run a vehicle by arranging to give him 30,000 £1 Preference shares in his company, McVitie & Price. The interest from the shares was to be used solely for the purchase and upkeep of a motor car — a Daimler — and the shares were to revert to Grant or his son on MacDonald's death. When this arrangement became public knowledge it caused such a political storm that it lapsed within a year.

Dr Edgar L. Collis, who also wrote in opposition to the expulsion, was a great friend of Ramsay MacDonald's. Collis was Medical Inspector of Factories in the Home Office and later was appointed to the Talbot chair of Preventive Medicine at the Welsh National School of Medicine at Cardiff. He was married to Principal Fairbairn's daughter Barbara, and he built the imposing dwelling, Tower House, in Prospect Terrace, as his Lossiemouth home.

Dr John S. Fairbairn, Wimpole Street specialist, consulting Obstetrician to St Thomas's Hospital in London, and later President of the Royal College of Obstetricians and Gynaecologists, was strongly opposed to the proceedings. He subsequently conducted a vigorous correspondence with *The Northern Scot* in an attempt to make his views on "l'affaire Ramsay MacDonald", as he termed it, more widely known. He was a son of Dr A.M. Fairbairn, first Principal of Mansefield College, Oxford, who built Blucairn at Stotfield in Lossiemouth in 1906 as his summer residence.

A.G. Jeans of Liverpool later became Sir Alexander Grigor Jeans and presented the handsome silver shield for competition among the veterans which graces the trophy cabinet today. He and his son Ronald signed both petitions to the Council. He was a Liverpool magistrate, chairman of the Reform Club in that city and managing director of the Liverpool *Daily Post and Mercury* and also *The Echo*. He was twice captain of Wallasey golf club, and later chairman of the Press Association. Educated at Elgin Academy, he was the younger son of Robert Jeans who was proprietor of the old *Elgin Courier*.

R. Innes Cameron, captain in 1913-15, was staunchly on the side of fair play. His was a fairy-tale career, the wine merchant's apprentice who, by sheer hard work, went on to become one of the most prominent distillers in Scotland and chairman for many years of the Scottish Malt Distillers Association. His home was at Southview, Elgin, and from there his daughter Hilda launched a number of determined attacks on the

Scottish Ladies' Amateur Championship which eluded her in the end of the day, although she invariably acquitted herself with great distinction.

James Hay Glennie, a prominent Lossiemouth and Elgin lawyer, was appointed the first Town Clerk, Treasurer and Collector when Lossiemouth became a burgh in 1894. Apart from his busy legal practice he was a very successful farmer at Ardivot. He had attended Drainie school with Ramsay MacDonald and they remained firm friends throughout their lives. There can be little doubt where his sympathies lay.

John Foster, captain in 1915-17 and Sheriff Clerk of Morayshire since 1901, had himself, according to Ivall, been carpeted by the Elgin Club on more than one occasion. The Elgin Club, founded in 1864, was for the ease and comfort of gentlemen, and John (or Jock as he was known) Foster had behaved on occasion in a less than gentlemanly manner. This was loosely defined as "improper behaviour" and he had received several final warnings from the committee. Perhaps MacDonald's letter about the Council's duty being "to preserve sobriety in the clubhouse" had found its mark. Foster later became secretary of the Moray Golf Club and was to send out notices of special meetings aimed at reinstatement of the member he had played such a prominent part in expelling.

John Foster was a stocky man with a smooth manner and a sharp tongue and stories about him still circulate. When the annual subscription was small a rather irate member arrived at the club house and demanded to see the secretary. "Do you realise, Sir," he said to Foster "that there are daisies growing on the seventeenth green?" "What the hell do you expect for two guineas" growled Foster, "Orchids?"

John Foster

On another occasion he was playing golf with a small friend who lost his ball in the tall dense whins on the right of the second fairway and after a fruitless search found he had lost his partner too. "Foster", he shouted, and received a tap on the shoulder. "Ah" said Foster, "Dr Livingstone I presume." It is said of him that every time he passed the poor-house in Elgin he doffed his hat and exclaimed "one never knows". He died in 1946 at the age of 76 — but not in the poor-house. He was the author of *The Bright Eyes of Danger* (a story of the 1745 Jacobite rebellion) published in March 1916, which went through five editions, *The Searchers,* and a number of short stories. He was also a contributor to the *St Andrews Treasury of Scottish Verse* which was edited and produced by the first captain, Professor Alexander Lawson. When Foster's large English sheepdog Caesar died he was buried on the last hole of the Relief course — the seventeenth of the New course today. The hole is still called "Caesar's Grave".

The enigmatic London barrister Lewis Noad was to find himself the object of much of the hostility of those who were opposed to the expulsion, particularly in Lossiemouth. At the time of these events Lewis Noad was fifty years of age and a practising barrister in Admiralty and Commercial courts. He had led a varied and exciting life, going to sea in 1880 at fifteen years of age trading round Cape Horn and South America for two years in a small sailing vessel, then in the large Calcutta sailing clipper *Benvenue*. Later he sailed the world with the Pacific & Orient Company and became a master mariner. He was called to the bar at Lincoln's Inn in 1896 and later took silk. Apart from the Moray Golf Club he was a member of the Reform Club and Coombe Hill golf club.

The Second Special Meeting
The first attempt to overturn the resolution was made eight years later when Ramsay MacDonald had become Prime Minister for the first time. At a Council meeting on 17th April 1924 the antipathy to MacDonald surfaced again when John F. Cumming suggested that the Council might recommend to the annual meeting that the expulsion be rescinded *simpliciter*, and the question of rejoining the club left to MacDonald. Colonel W.J. Johnston supported this, but the feeling of the Council was that the initiative, as before, should come from the members.

At this Special meeting in the Burgh Court House, Elgin, on 25th July 1924, presided over by the captain, A. Low Mustard, a prominent Elgin solicitor, the motion in favour of reinstatement was put by the Rev. W. E. Shaw, Lossiemouth, and seconded by John Sim, retired draper, Lossiemouth. The direct negative was moved by D. Macpherson, Tan Works, Elgin, and seconded by Captain G. E. Gordon Duff of Hopeman Lodge.

In the ensuing discussion Major F. Bennett wished to refer to statements made by Ramsay MacDonald at the outbreak of war, but the chairman ruled him out of order. During the Rev. Shaw's speech Dr T.H.W. Alexander of Elgin asked permission to protest against certain of his statements but Shaw refused to give way. The vote was then taken by ballot. Two members abstained, but fifty-five voted in favour of the motion and forty-five against, a majority of ten in favour of reinstatement. Since the constitution required a two-thirds majority the motion was defeated and the Prime Minister of Great Britain remained *persona non grata* at the Moray Golf Club in his native Lossiemouth.

The following day *The Manchester Guardian* announced that the Prime Minister had accepted the Freedom of the City of Edinburgh. A number of London newspapers carried the story that a wealthy member of the Moray Golf Club and an admirer of the Prime Minister who lent the club £3000 without interest had demanded that the money be repaid. This prompted an editorial in *The Guardian* headed "The Nineteenth Hole".

> Lossiemouth Golf Club is finding that the nineteenth is much the most difficult hole on its pleasant course. It stuck manfully to its guns in excluding a member named MacDonald because it disapproved of his tactics on that green. Even the fact that he was later appointed Prime Minister of the kingdom did not alter its decision.
> A man, it said to itself, whose views on the taxation of land values, for instance, are as appalling as Mr MacDonald's cannot be an acceptable member of our club. Let England think what it likes about him, Lossiemouth Golf Club's opinion is unchanged. His golf may be tolerable and his manner pleasant, but on the nineteenth green we will not have him. Who knows but that he might instil into the very caddies a spirit

Ramsay MacDonald arriving at Lossiemouth Station — 1925

of unrest which would lead them to confiscate lost balls without compensating the owners? Premier or no Premier, away with him! said the Lossiemouth Club, and at least it was consistent.

But now, it appears, a sort of economic vengeance has descended on these logicians, for a capitalistic member who seems to have enjoyed Mr MacDonald's company, even on the nineteenth green, and to whom incidentally the club owes a trifle of three thousand pounds lent without interest, proposes to call in his money by way of protest.

We do not doubt that the Lossiemouth Golf Club diehards, consistent to the end, will easily find the cash. But it is surely an amazingly wry conception of club life that compels them to do so. If the Prime Minister could be fairly charged with concealing his true handicap, if he were even dimly suspected of grounding his club in a bunker, or if, sin of sins, he refused to talk golf interminably, even at the nineteenth hole, and insisted on sketching a plan for the pacification of Europe when he ought by all the canons to be explaining with a wealth of detail why he did not get down in four at the tenth, the soul of every golfer would endorse the Lossiemouth Club's decision.

But Mr MacDonald is charged with none of these crimes; and there is, therefore, a certain satisfaction for all golfers in the amusing economic situation that follows on his expulsion. It may at least serve to remind the sturdy politicians who will be inconvenienced by it that even a member so deluded as to believe that all is not yet accomplished in improving upon this best of all possible worlds is nevertheless quite acceptable, even at the nineteenth hole, if in other respects he plays the game.

George Bernard Shaw, holidaying in Grantown-on-Spey, was interviewed by *The Strathspey Herald* on the subjects of Grantown and the Moray Golf Club. Shaw declined to discuss either topic, but sat down and wrote this characteristic message:

My business in this neighbourhood is to visit Lossiemouth. I felt I must see a place which has simultaneously produced the best Prime Minister of my time and the most stupendous collection of golf snobs known to history. Both should have a monument there.

There is reason to believe that tentative approaches had been made to Ramsay MacDonald about rejoining the golf club in 1922 and these may have been prompted by [Sir] Alexander Grant, Ramsay's friend and wealthy benefactor to the golf club. Malcolm MacDonald wrote a long letter to his father from The Queens College, Oxford, on January 19th 1923, which contained the following paragraph.

....I should think it would be a good thing if you decided to go back into the Moray Golf Club, provided they made a complete apology and withdrawal of their action. You would find the benefit of golfing again, and we could re-gather most of the clubs. In a way it is better to refuse negotiation altogether; but it would probably disappoint Foster and Co. most if you did go back. There are more than sufficient friends there to make that crowd feel small whenever you appeared on the premises. I hope that you are having a good holiday in Lossiemouth.

Malcolm MacDonald

If the Moray Golf Club thought that this was the last brush with the MacDonald family they were sadly mistaken. In the *Sunday Post* of September 5th 1926, amidst reports of the miners' strike, the front page carried the headline "Moray Golfers And Ex-Premier's Son — Mr MacDonald On Missing Letter". The report datelined "Lossiemouth (Saturday Night)" was as follows.

Owing to the great secrecy maintained by the Moray Golf Club, Lossiemouth, in regard to the reporting of Mr MacDonald for alleged breaches of the rules, it is impossible to say what the relationship really is between the club and the ex-Premier's son. Golfers who are in a good position to know, assert that a letter was sent to Mr Malcolm MacDonald, informing him that he had been reported for cutting in at the second and the eleventh tees, and calling for an expression of regret or his resignation. The mysterious part of the matter is that the letter has never reached its destination.

Mr MacDonald himself is greatly puzzled. "I wrote last night", he said, "to the secretary of the club, telling him that I was popularly supposed to have been called upon to resign or apologise, but that the letter to this effect had never reached me. I should imagine that it could only be addressed to me at my father's house here, and letters do not usually vanish into the void in Lossiemouth."

"There is a strong feeling amongst the rank and file," said Mr David West, R.S.W., the Scottish seascape painter, who is a prominent member of the club, "that no exception should be made in the case of Mr Malcolm MacDonald simply because he happens to be the son of an ex-Prime Minister. If Mr MacDonald refuses or neglects to apologise, there can be no other course than to ask for his resignation."

It would truly be a remarkable state of matters if both Mr Ramsay MacDonald and his son were debarred from membership of the same club in the former's native town. Meanwhile the mystery of the letter remains unsolved, and Malcolm MacDonald himself continues to divide his holiday between the courses at Lossiemouth and Spey Bay.

At a Council meeting in Elgin on 6th September, Low Mustard informed the members of reports which had appeared in *The People's Journal, The Sunday Post, The Glasgow Herald, The Bulletin* and *The Scotsman*. The captain said that the bulk of these articles was made up of inaccurate statements. Malcolm MacDonald had not been reported to the committee and no letter had been sent to him by the secretary. His own name had been made use of and he (Low Mustard) had received a letter

A. Low Mustard

from Malcolm MacDonald. As the matter concerned the club as well as himself, he thought it advisable to submit his proposed reply to MacDonald.

Elgin
6th September 1926

Dear Sir,

    Mr A. Low Mustard, the Captain of the Club, has handed me your letter of 3rd inst. addressed to him, and has asked me to reply on behalf of himself and the Council of the club.

    Mr Mustard cannot understand why you should think that his authority is being given for spreading the tale. The fact is quite the reverse as may be seen from the Press Reports and the enclosed copy letter which he wrote to the Editor of *The People's Journal* on Friday last, 3rd inst., to which as yet no reply has been received.

    Neither the Council nor the Officials of the Club have written any letter such as you refer to, nor have they any knowledge of such a letter.

Yours faithfully,
John Foster
Secretary.

Malcolm MacDonald Esq.,
"The Hillocks"
Lossiemouth.

The secretary reported that MacDonald had broken the rules but that no communication had been sent to him. It was agreed that the letter drafted by Low Mustard should be sent to MacDonald and no statement given to the press. No more was to be heard of this curious affair.

Reinstatement

Ramsay MacDonald was Prime Minister for the second time when the long awaited reinstatement took place at the same Burgh Court House in Elgin on 11th July 1929 at yet another special meeting, attended by ninety-nine members. This meeting was of quite a different order. The motion referred to "The Right Honourable James Ramsay MacDonald M.P. having been deprived of his membership" and the Press — excluded from the meeting as usual — reported the attendance of members from as far as Aberdeen on the one side and Inverness on the other, as well as visitors to Lossiemouth from the south who were members of the club.

The motion for reinstatement was moved by J.D.Taylor, captain of the club, and seconded by John F. Cumming, Convener of Morayshire, and twice captain of the golf club. According to *The Courant* both speeches were loudly applauded. An Elgin member who moved that the Premier should not only be reinstated but sent an apology was ruled out of order. Colonel W.J. Johnston of Elgin moved that no ballot be taken and this was seconded by Robert Tulloch, schoolmaster, Lossiemouth. A show of hands clearly demonstrated that everyone was in favour of rescinding the resolution. The unanimous decision was received with very loud applause.

J.D. Taylor

A well-known member informed *The Courant* reporter that all the members present seemed to realise the huge mistake that had been made in 1916 and were out to make amends as far as possible. "We only hope that Mr MacDonald will accept membership, and that one day he will honour us by becoming President of the club."

Lord Provost Wittet of Elgin thought that the meeting was particularly representative and he was only too pleased about the outcome. He himself had voted in the minority twice previously. Another member interviewed asserted that if the same common sense and sportsmanship had been in evidence in 1916, Mr MacDonald would never have been expelled. He felt that the Prime Minister would be welcomed with open arms when he again played on the course, the freedom of which should never been denied him.

In its Editorial next day *The Courant* commented.

It is sufficient that the Moray Golf Club has made full amends for what happened in 1916, and with the healing process that time generally effects, Mr MacDonald no doubt will reciprocate the friendly feeling manifested by the Club at its meeting last night. All sensible people recognised the anomalous situation created by the fact that a distinguished statesman of this country, of whom Lossiemouth in particular is rightly proud, who has been twice entrusted by the King with the Premiership, who is a freeman of many great cities of Britain, and who has been elected a member of the most exclusive club in London, the Athenaeum, was not considered good enough to be a member of the Golf Club of his native town. This reproach is happily now removed, and the Club is to be congratulated on the wisdom and justice of the decision to which it has now unanimously come.

Low Mustard's view, that it was quite conceivable that Ramsay MacDonald might decline to accept reinstatement, which would mean a loss of dignity to the club, was fully realised. There was to be no reciprocation of friendly feelings — and indeed no response. The bird had long since flown.

The following correspondence had taken place between the Laird of Pitgaveny and his friend Ramsay MacDonald prior to the special meeting.

> Pitgaveny, Elgin, Scotland.
> June 28th 1929.
>
> My dear Premier,
>
> ....I was home wounded in 1916 and raised my voice loud against the then action of the Club. I have thus taken a consistent line throughout which makes walking easy. I take it that you must be privy to what is going on, for knowing the character of my J.R. MacD. as I do, I feel certain he is just the man to tell them to "go to hell". I would also.
>
> Anyhow, don't bother to answer this UNLESS you wish me to act for you: if I don't hear I'll leave the idiots who made the mess to d----d well lick it up.
>
> Yours aye,
> J.B.Dunbar

> Captain J.B. Dunbar,
> Pitgaveny, Elgin
>
> Monday 1st July 1929
>
> My dear Laird,
>
> Thank you so much for your letter and its enclosure. [Notice of the meeting]. I want the members to be left absolutely alone and to consider nothing but what they feel it is their duty to do regarding the existence of the banning resolution. As a matter of fact I do not come into it at all. They have had any number of opportunities to put things right within the last few years, and once they definitely declined to do so. Now, everybody laughs at them and the existence of the resolution humiliates them, not me. What they are therefore proposing to do is get themselves out of a fix...
>
> I enjoy the Spey Bay course and so do my friends. It came to my rescue in 1916 and I am not a man to treat any friends of mine as a mere convenience. Therefore I stick to Spey Bay.
>
> Yours sincerely,
> J. Ramsay MacDonald

The Prime Minister at Spey Bay

An interesting light on the affair is that no other resignations are recorded apart from those of Sir Roderick Wigan and H.V. Masefield in October 1915. Among the new members admitted after the resignations were Mrs Romney Faris, The Craig, Lossiemouth, Mrs Maude Holdsworth of St Johns Wood, London, David C. Blair of Leighton Manse, Dunblane, and L. Davidson of York House, Cullen. M.A. Macfeat, Dr John Anderson and Dr Farquhar Macrae, all of Glasgow, became members in March 1916 and the latter was soon to be one of the thirty signatories to the second petition. Mrs Philip Hills of London and the Hon. Nesta Douglas-Pennant of Hall Place, Hants, became members six weeks before MacDonald was expelled.

It seems unlikely that Ramsay MacDonald's golfing companions caused any offence. Newspaper reports state that he played frequently — often daily — with Herbert Asquith, the Prime Minister, up to the outbreak of War. MacDonald's guests on the links, and in the clubhouse, included W.R.Gourlay, I.C.S., private secretary to the Governor of Bengal, Provost Archibald of Buckie, the Rev. R. Kemp of Blairgowrie, and the Rt. Hon. T. Mackinnon Wood, Secretary of State for Scotland in 1912. The local doctors, Clark and Brander, and R.I. Cameron were regular golfing partners. All seem to have rubbed shoulders with other members and visitors of the time — Lord Walter Gordon Lennox, Major General Lord Cheylesmore, K.C.V.O., of Easter Elchies, Captain the Hon. W. Chetwynd, Mrs Sassoon and Leopold and Leonard Rothschild from Tulchan Lodge on Speyside, Sir Symon Fortescue, Sir John Hewett, G.C.S.I., and officers from H.M.S. *Lion, Prince George, Collingwood* and *Shannon,* when Battle Cruiser Squadrons of the Fleet were in the neighbourhood.

Seventy-three of the 564 members of the golf club had voted for the expulsion of Ramsay MacDonald. However, none of the 239 lady members were present at the special meetings as ladies were not granted the vote in the Moray Golf Club until long after the second world war. Much good the suffragettes did them.

The following verses are attributed to Harry Simpson, who was a local poet of some renown in Elgin.

"CONDOLENCE."

A Satire on the refusal of the Moray Golf Club, on 25th July, 1924, to rescind the motion passed on 1st September, 1916, expelling from Membership of the Club the Right Hon. J. Ramsay MacDonald, Prime Minister.

Dear Ramsay MacDonald,
Nae doot ye'll alloo'
You're feelin' gae sma'
An' doon in the moo
Since the voice o' the mighty-
Staunch patriots a'-
Has again put a ban
On your game at the ba'.

In motors they cam'
Ay, a hunner or mair-
The flooers (?) o' the Coonty
Were a' gethert there
Determined to stan'
By their motion or fa'
In tryin' tae stop
Your wee game at the ba'.

52

Some gallants amang them-
　　Their names dinna speir,
　　But durin' the war
They kept well tae the rear-
Noo showed they had mettle,
　　An' led the attack-
　　An' Ramsay puir chiel,
　　You're nae gettin' back.

Ye may handle wi' skill
The sma' things o' the State;
Ye may strive to bring peace
　　Amang nations wha hate;
　　Hob-nob wi' your King,
　　An' play ither high jinks,
But you'll no play at gouf
　　On your ain Lossie links.

There the saut o' the earth
　　Play a dignified game;
Being men o' great minds
　　They a' think the same.
But ye dared to haud views
On what's richt and wrang
Quite different frae theirs,
　　So you'll jist hae to gang.

Na, na, you're nae fit
　　To breathe the same air
Wi' sodgers like Noad,
Wha wad do and wad dare.
　　Dire, dire is your fate,
　　An' dark your ootlook-
Noo there's only Spey Bay
　　An' a game wi' the Duke.*

* The Duke of Richmond and Gordon at Gordon Castle, Fochabers

There *is* a monument to Ramsay MacDonald at Lossiemouth and a plaque on the house where he was born in the Seatown. If there is a monument to Shaw's "stupendous collection of golf snobs" it is the clubhouse and the golf courses at Stotfield. In August 1929, the Rt. Hon. James Ramsay MacDonald, Prime Minister of Great Britain, was given the Freedom of the City of Elgin.

In his book *The (Ab)use of Power,* James Margach has this to say of Ramsay MacDonald.

Of all the Prime Ministers in this gallery MacDonald has had the rawest deal from history. He has received inadequate recognition as one of the powerful influences in shaping the twentieth century largely because he was the earliest victim of the vogue for "instant history", being used then as the ready-made peg on which to hang myths and legends now sanctified in Labour's folklore. He was that odd combination of realist and idealist, one moment a mob orator and spellbinder, the next the organisation man. His achievements were substantial: he welded together an astonishing collection of groups, movements, splinters and committees into the Labour Party, and then became Prime Minister three times. As Harold Macmillan said of his old adversary: "The first Labour Government was a remarkable achievement. MacDonald had brought a party to power in a single generation and himself to the highest office... His life must be judged whole." The verdict of A.J.P. Taylor: "He had, in some undefined way, the national stature which other Labour men lacked. He was maybe vain, solitary; yet, as Shinwell has said, in presence a prince among men. He was the last beautiful speaker of the Gladstone school, with a ravishing voice and turn of phrase... he dominated that movement as long as he led it."

It has been said that he was a man possessed with pride over the trappings and rewards of power. As someone who knew him from my days as a cub reporter I can discount this. One brief story illustrates the point. I was with him in his private sitting-room at No. 10 in 1935 when he returned from the Palace on resigning as Prime Minister. In answer to my query, he replied: "Yes, the King pressed me to accept an earldom. But I refused. Me an Earl? How ridiculous." Or the Garter? "Certainly not. When my time comes I'll be buried with my ain folk in the Spynie kirkyard as plain Jamie MacDonald, as I started, with no nonsense about titles." Not the response one would expect from someone supposedly consumed with pride and, without naming names, one can think of no other Labour leaders who showed any hesitation in laying their hands on an earl's ermine and a knight's garter.

CHAPTER V

Golf and Golfers at Lossiemouth

IT has been said earlier that things were never to be the same after the Second World War. The presence of a large military aerodrome on land adjoining the course was not a problem until Group Captain (later Air Commodore) [Sir] Frank Whittle invented the jet engine.

During the war Lossiemouth was a Royal Air Force station providing fully-trained bomber crews for Bomber Command and Group Captain Guy Gibson V.C., of Dam Buster fame, is said to have walked his dog on the beach at Lossiemouth. The aerodrome and the adjoining beaches were inspected in August of 1940 by General Sir Alan Brooke (later Field-Marshal Lord Alanbrooke) who had taken part in the Dunkirk evacuation and was then entrusted with command of the Forces preparing to repel the expected German invasion. Several famous missions started from Lossiemouth and in November 1944 a squadron of Lancasters took off to sink the German battleship *Tirpitz* in a Norwegian fiord.

[But] it was the fog-free climate and the generally fine weather in the Moray Firth which made Lossiemouth ideal for air crew training with less interruption than almost any other part of the British Isles, and the cream of Empire youth arrived to train on the way to battles over Europe. The Fleet Air Arm of the Royal Navy became the tenants as H.M.S. *Fulmar* in 1946, remaining until 1972 when the station reverted to the Royal Air Force. The Germans did not come, and neither so far have the Russians, and now our aircrew fly to sharpen their ability to deter potentially aggressive naval forces in the North Sea.

After the Second World War Lossiemouth declined as a holiday resort, partly because of the motor car and later, the advent of cheaper and faster air travel which guaranteed a seaside holiday [in Europe] with continuous sunshine. But largely it has to be said because of the noise of aircraft on some days and the occasional low flying over the beach and golf course. A dismissive article in a *Golf World* publication of 1985 entitled *The World of Scottish Golf* purporting to be *the* reference book for anyone contemplating a golfing holiday in Scotland did no justice at all to the two fine eighteen hole courses at Lossiemouth but fortunately did not deter our visitors nor our knowledgeable American friends. The flying is far from continuous but the co-operation of the Royal Air Force leaves something to be desired, particularly when the golf club is staging one of its major events and sufficient advance warning has been given to senior officers.

The Courses

The Old course is among the finest in Scotland. It is the equal of Dornoch and slightly more difficult than Nairn, and with somewhat similar histories, all three have enjoyed a friendly relationship which continues to the present day. The New course is also a considerable test of a golfer's ability, especially when a stiff breeze is blowing, and the dense whins lining some fairways have ruined many a good score.

Old Tom Morris, the St Andrews professional, was a frequent visitor to the north and played a prominent part in advising on the layout of such courses as Tain, Dornoch, Nairn and Lossiemouth. In April 1890 he came to inspect and play over the eighteen hole course at Lossiemouth. He travelled from Elgin with club officials in a brake which took forty-five minutes to reach the Stotfield links, while a large number of golfers arrived by train to watch the play. Tom Morris and John MacLeod, Her Majesty's Inspector of Schools, played the captain, Dr G.H. Mackay and the Rev. Alexander Lawson and beat them on the eighteenth green. At the conclusion Tom expressed himself well pleased with the progress that had been made, and gave it as his opinion that the course would be the best in the north. The members and spectators enjoyed the exhibition and the newspaper reports did not bear out Young Tommy's unkindly criticism of his father made many years previously. *Golf Illustrated* in 1899 quoted his remark about his father that "He'd be a braw putter, gin' the hole were aye a yaird nearer 'im".

Old Tom Morris

56

Although Tom Morris was over seventy years of age in 1892, he returned to the Stotfield links in March to take part in another foursome with the club officials. In the evening he dined with the Council in the Station Hotel, Elgin, and agreed to stay another day and take part in a match for the benefit of the members. Tom's counsel was taken as to the treatment of the greens, and he expressed a very high opinion of the quality and condition of the extended links.

The Northern Counties Cup

In 1899 a letter was received from the Aberdeen golf club suggesting that a competition be established to be called "The Northern Counties Cup", based on the County Cup competition in East Lothian. The first competition was to be held on Balgownie links in the summer of 1900 and the second at Lossiemouth, and all interested clubs were invited to contribute two guineas towards the cup. The Moray Club took up the idea with great enthusiasm and their second team of David West, David Cameron, John F. Cumming and J. Mackenzie Forbes won the cup at Lossiemouth in 1901.

In the light of the large number of participating clubs in the present day, the entrants at Lossiemouth in 1901 make interesting reading.

Aberdeen Club	2 teams
Moray	3 teams
Aberdeen University	1 team
Aberdeen Teachers Club	1 team
Aberdeen Licensed Victuallers	1 team
Inverness Club	2 teams
Buckie Club (Strathlene)	1 team

Exhibition Matches

The Moray Golf Club has never had a problem in attracting the best players in spite of its remoteness. The earliest recorded exhibition match took place on 26th August 1901 with J.H. Taylor, the first English professional to win the Open Championship in 1894, and he played Charles Neaves. This was so successful it was repeated in 1902 with Sandy Herd, the Open Champion, and James Braid, each guaranteed £7 and their railway fares from wherever they were in Scotland, playing Archie Simpson of Aberdeen, "a glorious driver with a glorious swing", and Charles Neaves the Moray professional. The minutes record:

> There was exhibited the finest golf that has ever been seen on the Stotfield links. The prizes which were presented by members of the club and their friends were decided in the morning as follows : Braid 74, Herd 76, Neaves 82 and Simpson 83. In the afternoon the record of the green which was formerly held by Neaves with 74 was broken by Herd who accomplished the round in 72.

The reader should remember that these scores were accomplished while using either the gutta percha ball or the poor quality early Haskells, and hand-made hickory shafted clubs, far removed from the precisely engineered clubs and golf balls of today. Without water in the summer the course was dry as a bone with greens as keen as ice. Greenkeeping was in its infancy.

Vardon

Harry Vardon often visited Lossiemouth and in a famous match in 1907 finished all square on the eighteenth green when playing the best ball of two young members, William Christie Jnr. and the seventeen year-old George Thomson. The Council had asked Taylor to come to Lossiemouth with Vardon but balked at his fee of £15 plus £7 : 10/- expenses. Vardon was paid a total of £25 and Charlie Neaves received £3 for losing on the eighteenth hole in their morning exhibition match. Taylor, Braid and Vardon all made suggestions for improving the course during their visits, and these were invariably acted upon. At the McVitie and Price Professional Tournament of 1920 James Braid, Arnaud Massy, George Duncan and Ted Ray all met the captain J.F. Cumming for a long discussion on the Old course and suggested various alterations, although Ted Ray had been advising the Council for some years.

Other prominent professionals who played in competition at Lossiemouth include Tom Fernie, Sandy Herd, Jack White, Abe Mitchell, J.G. Sherlock, Tom Williamson, Jack Ross, Charles R. Smith, Archie Compston, Percy Alliss, Angel de la Torre, Tom Simpson, Frank Ball, Andrew Kirkaldy and Jean Gassiat of Chantilly.

The last exhibition match at Lossiemouth took place on 27th August 1949 and raised over £700 for the Scottish National Institution for War Blinded. Fred Daly (Open champion in 1947 and runner-up in 1948), Max Faulkner, Bill Shankland and Dai Rees were the participants, and Daly thrilled the large number of spectators by holing the course in sixty-three strokes. Obviously delighted by his performance, he told *The Elgin Courant* reporter: "This is one of the loveliest courses it has ever been my privilege to play over and it provides an excellent test even for the best of golfers. I only wish," he added, "that some of the big tournament golf which I have taken part in had been played over links such as this."

The Stotfield Hotel — 1900

Professional Tournaments

The Scottish Professional Golf Union applied to hold their fourth championship at Lossiemouth in 1910, to be decided by four rounds medal play over two days. The total prize money was £60 of which the club would contribute half. The Council were obviously pleased by the recognition of the course as a championship links and readily agreed, and the professionals were made honorary members of the club, with automatic entry to the clubhouse, during the time they were to be in Lossiemouth. The Moray Golf Club had a rather more enlightened approach to professional golfers than most golf clubs. All competitors were admitted to honorary membership of the club for amateur or professional events, whereas at Deal, in the Open Championship of 1920, Walter Hagen was driven to protest at the exclusion of professionals from the clubhouse by arriving in a chauffeur-driven limousine and using it as a changing room in full view of the clubhouse windows.

In what appears to be an early form of sponsorship in 1910, the Scottish Professional Golf Union made arrangements with the railway companies for cheap fares for the players, and William Christie of the Stotfield Hotel arranged for a reduced tariff for all professionals taking part.

Thirty-seven competitors took part as against sixty-two in the previous year's championship in 1909, and this was attributed to the inaccessibility of Lossiemouth and the fact that the course was an unknown quantity to many of them. The championship was played in glorious weather and the winner was Tom Fernie of Troon with 291 — fifteen strokes ahead of W. Binnie of Kinghorn, Fife. The feature of the play was Fernie's second round of 65 which broke the course record of 70 established by the Moray amateur George Thomson three weeks earlier. Seventy-nine years on from that distant day, and many modifications of the course later, no amateur or professional golfer has equalled Tom Fernie's score of 65 in a medal round.

THE MORAY GOLF CLUB.

Competition *Scottish Professional Cham- pionship (Open)*

Mr *J. R. O. Fernie*

Bogey.	Names of Holes.	Yds.	Strokes.
3	1. Mt. Lebanon - - -	216	3
5	2. Cup - - - - - -	426	5
5	3. Table - - - - -	421	3
4	4. Coulart - - - -	206	4
5	5. Kinneddar - - -	420	4
3	6. Gordonstoun - - -	130	3
5	7. Ring - - - - -	459	4
5	8. Heather - - - -	433	4
4	9. Ditch - - - - -	290	3	33
4	10. St. Gerardine - -	266	3
4	11. Lighthouse - - -	271	3
4	12. Beacon - - - -	305	4
5	13. V - - - - - -	466	4
5	14. Sea - - - - - -	263	4
3	15. Short - - - - -	166	2
5	16. Road - - - - -	372	4
5	17. Long - - - - -	490	4
5	18. Home - - - - -	400	4
78		6000	32

TOTAL 65

HANDICAP .... —

HANDICAP SCORE 65

59

THE "LADY'S PICTORIAL" GOLF COMPETITION, 1912:

THE EAST OF SCOTLAND QUALIFYING ROUND, PLAYED AT LOSSIEMOUTH, JUNE 10TH.

1. Miss K. Stuart, winner of the Scratch Division last year, again qualifies.   2. The 18th green.   3. Miss C. Kinloch, who qualifies with Miss Stuart in the Scratch Division.
4. Miss Glover putting on the 4th green.   5. On the 17th green.   6. Going to the 6th green.   7. Miss Neill Fraser, the divisional manager, on the 14th tee.   8. The 18th
green, showing the club house in the background.   9. Miss Savory, who qualifies for final in the 1st Handicap Division.   10. A group of competitors.   11. Mrs. Fyfe, who, with
Miss Savory, qualifies in the 1st Handicap Division.

Lossiemouth did not have long to wait for a second championship, and in 1912 the Scottish Ladies' Amateur Championship was played over the links. The Great War put paid to the possibility of attracting other major events, but once it was over, Alexander Grant of Edinburgh quickly showed his generosity to the club by sponsoring the McVitie & Price Professional Tournament at Lossiemouth on 1st, 2nd and 3rd June 1920, with prize money of over £550. McVitie & Price was the very successful Scottish biscuit firm owned by Grant and a top class field was guaranteed with this amount of money at stake. The first prize was £100, with many other handsome prizes, and although this may seem trifling in relation to today's massive sums it should be remembered that £3 was a good weekly wage in 1920. George Smith, the professional in 1920, had a retainer of £1 per week and the head greenkeeper received £2 : 5/- as a weekly wage.

An international match was played on Tuesday, 1st June 1920, and England won by two holes. The tournament proper began on Wednesday 2nd June after a night of rain which left the greens slow, but there was no wind and conditions must have been benign for a seaside links. St Andrew, patron saint of golf, smiled on the local professional George Smith on the first day and he returned cards of 73 and 72 which led the field by two shots. George Duncan and Abe Mitchell were on 147, James Braid on 149 and Ted Ray on 151. Further down the field came Arnaud Massy, J.H.Taylor and Harry Vardon.

The second day was ideal for golf but the pressure proved too much for poor George Smith and he returned 89 and 81 to finish well down the field to the disappointment of his many supporters. He did not go away empty-handed as three guineas was awarded for the lowest score in each round, of which he had two, and he no doubt shared in the additional £100 which the sponsor decided to give to those not in the list of successful players.

James Braid (Walton Heath) and Abe Mitchell (North Foreland), with an aggregate score of 292, tied for the first place. Ted Ray (Oxhey) was third with 294, Arnaud Massy (Nivelle) fourth with 295, and George Duncan (Hangerhill) fifth with 296. Duncan was to win the Open Championship at Deal one month later. J.B. Batley (Royal Flying Club) and Arnaud Massy established a new record of 70 for the altered course.

Among those who shared in the additional prize money was the fifty-two year old Sandy Herd of Coombe Hill who opened with an 82 but pulled himself steadily up the field with rounds of 79, 77 and 72 to finish in a respectable seventeenth place and beat the fifty year-old Vardon by one shot. Andrew Kirkaldy (St Andrews) was the oldest competitor at sixty years of age and even if his lowest score was 82 he handed in cards for all four rounds played in the two days. Sandy Herd won the Open Championship once only, at Hoylake in 1902, when he shrewdly used the relatively new rubber-cored ball which had arrived from America while the other leading professionals played the gutta percha.

In 1921 H.S. Colt of Sunningdale, English international, scratch golfer and well-known golf course architect, was commissioned to alter the first and the sixth holes. He sent a telegram suggesting that his partner Dr Alister MacKenzie, who was to be forty miles distant at Macduff at the time, should make the inspection at Lossiemouth. The Council had never heard of Dr MacKenzie and replied that they would prefer Colt himself. Bobby Jones wrote of the designing of Augusta National in 1930, where the U.S. Masters is played in April of each year: "With this sort of land, of a soft,

61

gentle, rather than spectacular beauty, it was especially appropriate that we chose Dr Alister MacKenzie to design our course."

Without his famous partner, Harry Colt proposed a major alteration to the first hole which was speedily approved of by the Council and carried out by the green staff. It was then a blind, tricky short hole of 216 yards played over a long high bank, known as Mount Lebanon, with a vast natural sand bunker on its face. This was transformed into a good opening hole of 350 yards by moving Mount Lebanon thirty yards to the south where it stands to the present day, and building a new tee nearer the clubhouse. This was effected with barrows and shovels and one horse and cart: surely a prospect to make even the stoutest greenkeeper quail. A new tee was also built and the greenkeeper was instructed to "put a man on duty at the first hole from noon until dark to prevent mischief on Sundays, the man to be allowed 5/- a day". This was a necessary precaution as the public have access to the links and mischief is not uncommon in the present day.

The McVitie & Price Tournament was again held at Lossiemouth in 1922 with a handsome new trophy plus prize money of £800, and once more all the big names were present with the exception of Braid and Taylor. Aubrey Boomer (St. Cloud) the French champion, Ray, Vardon, Mitchell, Duncan, Ockenden, Gadd and a host of other prominent professionals were present on the practice day. The first prize was £130, whereas the winner of the British Open Championship at Sandwich that year, Walter Hagen, received £75 and in the most famous of all Hagen gestures handed it straight to his elderly caddie Daniels. When Hagen won his next Open two years later at Hoylake he is reputed to have supplemented the still meagre first prize by winning a bet of £3000 on himself.

The opening day's play on Monday the 15th June was marred by steady rain but J.H. Kirkwood (Australia) broke the record for the altered course with a 69 in the first round. A round of 77 in the afternoon, and two steady rounds of 72 apiece on the Tuesday gave him a total of 290 and won him the splendid new cup and the first prize of £130 by a margin of thirteen strokes. Fine golfer though he was, Joe Kirkwood later became more famous for his skill as a trick shot artist, and he travelled the world giving exhibitions with Walter Hagen. Runners-up on 303 were the Aberdonian George Duncan (Hangerhill) and L. Holland (Church Brampton) who each collected £65. The 25 year-old Percy Alliss (father of Peter), playing out of his first club Clyne at Swansea, returned 317 and won £10.

Joe Kirkwood's caddie was Jimmie Main of Lossiemouth who, at the age of ninety, recalls his employer vividly. Walking down one fairway on the inward half Kirkwood remarked that the skyline and the clubhouse reminded him of St Andrews, but he thought that Moray was a far better golf course. His 69 — out in 31 and back in 38 — may well have encouraged him in this view. His caddie could have expected elevenpence a round but to his utter astonishment he received twenty pounds from the winner's cheque.

Over the years Jimmie Main remembers caddying for many fine golfers at Lossiemouth — Dorothy Campbell who won the British Ladies' in 1909 and the first of two women golfers to win the British, American and Canadian Championships; the illustrious Joyce and Roger Wethered who were frequent guests of the Tennants at Innes House; Bridget Newell, the youngest barrister in England and runner-up to Pam Barton in the British Ladies' of 1936, and Jack McLean who won the Northern Open Championship at Lossiemouth in 1937. McLean had been beaten by a cruel stymie at the thirty-fourth hole in the final of the 1936 American Amateur Championship at Garden City, New York, when he had looked certain to become dormie on Johnny Fischer, and lost the match at the thirty-seventh hole. No wonder Jimmie remembers McLean as one of the best iron players he ever saw.

The Scottish Ladies' Amateur Championship returned to the Moray course in 1923 and was played there for the third time in 1935. In 1925 the Scottish professionals decided to play their fifteenth championship at Lossiemouth and the Council agreed to subscribe £50 towards the prize fund. In addition £150 of prize money was contributed by McVitie and Price, the company owned by Sir Alexander Grant who followed the play closely, while Lady Grant presented the prizes on the final day. According to *The Northern Scot,* they were staying at the Marine Hotel with their son Robert, as were the rest of the party which had accompanied the ex-Prime Minister, the Rt. Hon. James Ramsay MacDonald, and his daughter Ishbel to Lossiemouth for the Whitsuntide Parliamentary recess.

Among the party at Lossiemouth were the Earl and Countess de la Warr, General Lord Thomson (later to be lost over France in 1930 in the wreck of the airship R 101), [Sir] Oswald Mosley with his wife, Lady Cynthia Mosley, John Strachey and the Lord Mayor of Bradford. Earl de la Warr's ancestor, Thomas, was colonial governor of Virginia in the seventeenth century, and the state of Delaware in the U.S.A. is named after him. *The Northern Scot* reported that the ex-Prime Minister and his party had spent the whole of their time playing golf at Spey Bay golf course where MacDonald had been made an honorary member after being expelled from the Moray Golf Club. Oswald Mosley was a political chameleon who was first a Conservative M.P. and then an Independent M.P. before joining the Labour party. He achieved notoriety when he founded the British Union of Fascists in 1931 and was interned in Holloway gaol in London from 1941-43.

This 1925 Scottish Championship was won by the Cruden Bay professional Stewart Burns with 297 and the runner-up was Tom Fernie of Turnberry with 302. The Moray professional George Smith was third, nine strokes behind the winner.

The Scottish Professional Championship returned to Lossiemouth in 1933 (the year of Meg Farquhar's baptism of fire) and was won by Mark Seymour of Crow Wood with an aggregate of 296, and when it returned in 1936 James Forrester of Cruden Bay was the champion with the excellent score of 287 which remained the record total for seventy-two holes at Moray for many years. John Campbell, of Lossiemouth and the Royal Aberdeen golf club, won the Scottish Championship over the course he was brought up on with a total of 292 in 1952. Since then, sponsorship of the "Tartan Tour" has meant that the professionals play their championship on an inland course in the central belt of Scotland.

The Northern Open

The Northern Scottish Open Championship has had a rather longer run at the Moray links and has produced much fine and entertaining golf. Jack McLean of Buchanan Castle won it with a total of 294 in 1937 and Eric Brown won the first of his five Northerns with a similar score in 1950. The championship was a very entertaining Brown/Panton benefit for many years and John Panton won for the fourth time in 1956 with a total of 290 at Lossiemouth. John Panton was a beautiful striker of a golf ball,

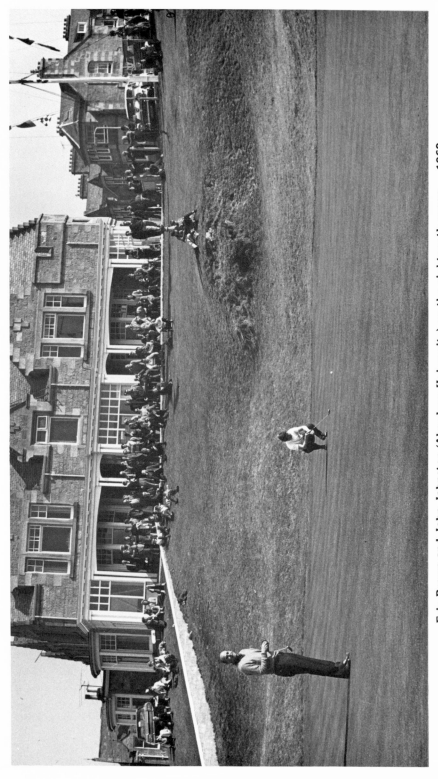

Eric Brown and John Johnston (Aberdeen University) on the eighteenth green — 1969

particularly with the medium irons, and he left himself with so many birdie opportunities that, had he been a really good putter, even his excellent record would have been a great deal better. He was a master of a seaside links in a strong wind, and in 1962 his last round of 69 in half a gale over the Moray course for a winning total of 300 can rarely have been bettered.

Harry Bannerman, chased all the way to the wire by John Panton, won by a whisker with 295 in 1969 at Lossiemouth when his drive at the eighteenth hole bounced off the top of the out-of-bounds wall back into the fairway to enable him to finish with a par four. The 1981 Northern Open at Lossiemouth was won by Alistair P. Thomson of Inverness with a total of 285, at that time the lowest four round total ever posted in a major competition at Moray and a full six shots better than Tom Fernie's total of 291 in the Scottish Professional Championship of 1910. A new record of 66 for the Old course was established by Tony Minshall (Hill Valley) who finished as runner-up, and this remains the record by a professional, or an amateur, in competition at Lossiemouth.

The most recent Northern Open at Lossiemouth was held in May 1988, and resulted in a fourth title win in fifteen years for David Huish of North Berwick. In doing so he set a new seventy-two hole record of 281 and equalled the course record of 66 in the very first round. Jock MacVicar of the *Scottish Daily Express* described the final round under the headline "Huish Money".

> David Huish won the £20,000 Clydesdale Bank Northern Open in a desperately tight finish at Lossiemouth yesterday with a three under par aggregate of 281. Only three weeks ago he failed to make the halfway "cut" at Dunbar, and after a record equalling 66 on the first day here he doubted if he was ready to win this week. "Deep down I'd be surprised to win," confessed the man who dominated the Tartan Tour before Jim Farmer and Russell Weir came along.
>
> But yesterday when the pressure played at least as great a part as technique, it was the Huish style which prevailed. He had European Tour players Mike Miller and Ian Young on his back for most of the final round, and until the closing moments a three-way play-off looked likely. But Miller bogeyed the long seventeenth, Young took a five at the last despite being given a free drop from a molehill, and behind the pair of them the P.G.A. captain calmly birdied the seventeenth.
>
> Now, at last, the situation was clear. Huish needed a par four at the last to win. The hole measures 423 yards, and with its bunkers on the left and line of rock gardens on the right, it has destroyed many a card. By this time however, Huish knew he could win, and he followed a perfect drive with an eight iron to within eighteen feet of the flagstick for the four and the 73 he required to pick up the £3,300 first prize. "Some would say I'm back, but I would say I've never been away," chuckled the champion after his one shot win over Miller.

His caddie, the strong and powerful local member Sandy Kinnaird, looked more drained than his employer, but no doubt he was equally satisfied.

It is interesting to note that the competitors and the attendant journalists alike reiterated what the author has maintained for years, that the Moray links is one of the best golf courses in Scotland. The golf correspondent of the *Scotsman* summed it up when he wrote "This is the seventh time the championship has visited the 6,643 yard Moray course, adjudged to be one of the finest tests on the Tartan Tour circuit."

Some Personalities

Augustus Thorne, who made his fortune as a merchant in China and the City of London, built the large house called Dunconusg on a site

David Huish putting out to win the 1988 Northern Open

overlooking the golf course in 1894. His widow was later made an honorary member of the golf club and it was from Dunconusg that the young Andrew Thorne began his long and happy association with the club. Andrew Thorne was to become a very distinguished soldier, winning no fewer than three Distinguished Service Orders in the First World War and ending the Second War as General Sir A.F.A.N. Thorne. He continued to return to fish the river Spey and play golf at Lossiemouth for many years and died while on holiday there in 1970. His life and achievements have been fittingly celebrated in a book by Donald Lindsay entitled *Forgotten General.* The two Messervys whose names appear on the War memorial in the clubhouse were cousins of Andrew Thorne. They were the sons of Mrs Thorne's sister and after the death of their father in 1893 and their mother in 1894 they were brought up as members of the Thorne family.

Many well-known Aberdeen golfers of an older generation played in the annual tournament or were members of the golf club. A host of Aberdeen doctors were members — Professor R.G. McKerron, F.K. (Fred) Smith the surgeon, Tom Robson the anaesthetist, Doctors John Elmslie and Norman Gadsby, Professor Sir Stanley Davidson who held the chair of medicine in Aberdeen until 1938 when he was translated to the chair of medicine in Edinburgh. Stanley Davidson became a distinguished President of the Royal College of Physicians in Edinburgh and continued to holiday in Lossiemouth until the 1970's, having been a member of the golf club for more years than he cared to remember. Professor Sir Dugald Baird of the chair of Obstetrics in Aberdeen could still recount to the author many years after it happened every shot of the best round he ever played, a sixty-nine over the links at Stotfield.

Douglas Dempster, a past captain of Royal Aberdeen golf club, has been visiting Lossiemouth and playing in the Moray Open for more than fifty years, and continues to encourage young Aberdeen golfers to follow his example. J.S.R. Cruickshank of Brander and Cruickshank has graced the Moray links on a number of occasions, and his partner E.W.H. Brander, a member for many years, spent holidays at the Stotfield Hotel and played golf daily in a four-ball which included George Smith, the Moray Club's professional.

George Wood ranks high among Lossiemouth members who are remembered for their golfing ability and sturdy independence. A banker with a keen wit and, at times, prickly personality, George was not afraid to speak his mind bluntly either in the Council chamber or on the golf course. Club champion seven times, he remained a first-class golfer to the end of his life. Never inclined to accept anything other than perfection, on one occasion he made no secret of the fact that he had moved the medal markers on one tee until they were aligned to his satisfaction during a competition, and when he was disqualified he expressed his disgust in no uncertain terms.

The period after the second war was notable for numerous forceful personalities, most of whom are sadly gone. J.C. (Doff) Thomson was a genial character both on and off the course who is remembered with affection by many. A very successful fisherman who had wisely opted in middle age for the safer field of marine insurance, he at last found himself with time to play golf and was the frequent organiser of an afternoon four-ball, or present ready to join in one. One of his more dramatic games involved himself as the principal player. Standing on the first tee one afternoon he complained to his companions of indigestion but proceeded to play some excellent golf in spite of the pain which spread upwards into his chest as the round progressed. On the ninth green he looked so ill that one of his partners offered to fetch a car and take him home but he refused this as he was playing so well. Somehow he completed his round in seventy-six strokes, sat down at the side of the eighteenth green and announced — "Now,— you can send for a doctor." He survived the heart attack which had begun on the first tee and played golf for many more years.

Another banker in David Cowper was never happier than when on the golf course. The winner of the club championship and of very many trophies, both at Lossiemouth and elsewhere, he was a determined and successful golfer who enjoyed the cut

J.C. (Doff) Thomson on the thirteenth tee

and thrust of matchplay. The ever present pipe and the little smile when he went one up on his opponent in a tough match are remembered by many. In common with all older golfers he lost length off the tee and through the green and he spent his later years in constant pursuit of theories or the one iron which might restore his youthful zest. David Cowper gave a great deal of his time to the administration of the golf club and was wholly committed to the furtherance of the excellence of the Moray Golf Club.

William J. Stewart was another post-war golfer whose name appears on many trophies and who was club champion on four occasions. An acknowledged expert on the rules of golf, he always represented his club throughout the north with great distinction.

CHAPTER VI

Greenkeeping

IT is difficult for golfers today to imagine the uneven character of a seaside links golf course one hundred years ago. In the very early years of the Moray Golf Club the grass was cropped by large numbers of rabbits, aided by sheep grazing on the course in the winter and spring time. Scythes were used to keep the longer, thicker grass under control and to clear areas around greens and tees. Many of the shingle banks on the course were uncovered and the stones were a permanent hazard. There were many sand wastes which, over a long period of years, were covered by soil and then turfed. Bunkers were introduced gradually and then filled in and replaced as the course was extended, and particularly as the golf ball travelled further with improved techniques for manufacturing both golf clubs and balls.

Shortly after his engagement as club professional in 1900, Charles Neaves was informed by the Council that, as well as visiting the links daily for purposes of examination, he should also go there early in the morning, at six o'clock if necessary, to satisfy himself that the men started work at the proper hour. Neaves was also to lodge a monthly report with the secretary with regard to the condition of the course with any suggestions for its improvement and giving dates of his early visits.

Eighty year-old William (Barney) Watson was a member of the greenkeeping staff at Lossiemouth from 1929-39. He recalls working from 7 a.m. to 5 p.m. for a weekly wage of forty-five shillings, without any increase in ten years, although there was always a bonus of £5 in July after the annual tournament. The green staff then consisted of four men and an apprentice who looked after twenty-seven holes and a small children's course of six holes. In 1928 the staff were Dugald Macdonald, greenkeeper, at £3 : 3/- a week, three men, Macdonald, Robertson and Reid at £2 : 5/- each per week, and Roy Cattell the apprentice at £1 : 5/- per week — a total wage bill of just over £11 per week.

Dugald Macdonald died in 1930 after twenty-two years as greenkeeper to the club and his son Stewart, who had been employed on the course since his boyhood, was one of forty-four applicants for the post. (This was a small number in comparison with more than three hundred and forty applicants for the vacant post of club steward in 1927). From a short list of three, D. Williamson of Lundin Links was excluded because it was felt he was too old at forty-four years of age. This left James Mackintosh of Dornoch, greenkeeper there and at Wiesbaden, where he was principal greenkeeper, and Stewart Macdonald of Lossiemouth. Mackintosh was prepared to accept a wage of £2 : 10/- but Macdonald was appointed to follow in his father's footsteps at £3 per week with rent and rate-free occupancy of Sunnyside Cottage, the greenkeeper's residence.

Members who are accustomed to the manicured courses of the present day should find the newly appointed greenkeeper's report of May 1930 of interest.

> The working hours are seven a.m. to twelve noon and one p.m. to five p.m. in summer, and daylight to dark in the winter. The greens are cut twice weekly, once by hand-mower and once by motor-mower, and each member of the staff has definite greens allotted to him to keep. The tees are cut once weekly, mostly by hand-mower, the larger ones by motor. The fairways generally are cut every two weeks and the reaper is in working order. It is recommended that soot be used as a dressing to improve the colour of the grass.

Soot is mentioned as a dressing for the greens as early as 1903 and it must have been infinitely preferable to the horse manure so often used at an earlier period. Barney Watson recalls cycling to the Lossiemouth chimney-sweeps to collect bags of soot which were taken to the green-sheds and mixed with beach sand, taken from the dunes, to provide a top-dressing for the greens in the Spring and Autumn. He also recalls being on night duty in dry spells in mid-summer when two men were engaged in watering the greens from ten o'clock at night until six o'clock in the morning. Each man had a barrow containing a hose and watered nine greens on the Old course, but the nine hole Relief course was rarely watered. New holes were cut on the greens twice weekly.

The greens were frequently rolled by hand with a five hundred-weight roller. Watson always used a hand-pushed mower with rollers to cut the greens, and as the mower had no box, the lumps of cut grass on wet greens had to be broken up with a bamboo cane switch. The Council had considered the purchase of a motor-mower for the greens in 1919 but did not proceed further after hearing from other golf clubs that the use of these mowers was not entirely satisfactory. Eventually, in June 1921, the club purchased its first "Atco" motor lawn-mower for cutting the greens, with the aid of a gift of £50 from a club member. In 1928, an anonymous donor, now known to be Francis Tennant of Innes House, presented the club with a Gun-Joey motor tractor at a cost of £145 from the D. & S. Autocar Co. Ltd., Manufacturing Engineers, London.

Mechanisation has seen great changes in greenkeeping practices, particularly in the last twenty years. Like so many other seaside links courses today, a watering system was installed on the Old course in 1983 at a cost of about £50,000. This was essential in view of the severe drought conditions which have prevailed in the past, but the application of water is controlled to preserve the seaside grasses and the hard, fast links greens. Compaction and thatching are problems which can be dealt with by recognition and adequate aeration. The large area of ground to be looked after by the green staff means that the most modern equipment in the form of tractors, gang-mowers, rough-cutters, and machines for slitting and hollow-tining the turf is in continuous use on both eighteen hole courses. Two modern triplex mowers are in use, one for the tees and one for the greens and surrounds. Robert Stronnar and Robert Scott, professionals and keepers of the green in the last century would be quite surprised.

70

CHAPTER VII

The Northern Amateur Championship at Lossiemouth

THE Northern Amateur championship was first played at Lossiemouth in 1894 and is one of the oldest amateur tournaments in the world. The first unofficial Open Championship of America — decided by matchplay — was held the same year and four players took part. From the outset the Northern Amateur — played today as the Moray Open Amateur — was a great success and in its first year attracted 111 entries, far in excess of the numbers entered for the British Amateur of 1894. Until the second war it attracted very talented young golfers from far and wide and many of them were to make their mark on the national and international scene.

In 1894 the competitors came from Dornoch in the north to London in the south and the large number of eager spectators surprised the organisers. They were described as a gay and carefree throng with the proper touch of colour in the red coats of the golfers and the summer costumes of the ladies. This first contest was decided by stroke play over thirty-six holes, and at the end of the day three players were tied for the cup on 170 — John Sutherland the Dornoch secretary, J.H. Andrew of Prestwick St Nicholas and L.W. Macpherson of Edinburgh. *The Elgin Courant* relates how the three champions stepped on to the first tee in a fever of excitement for the play-off over nine holes which was duly won by J.H. Andrew, and late in the evening the handsome trophy was presented to him by the captain, William Christie Snr. of the Station Hotel, Elgin. Even later in the evening rumours were current that something was up, and poor Andrew was asked to give back the cup. His partner in the stroke play was John Hunter the schoolmaster, and at one hole he had putted first and his ball knocked Andrew's ball into the hole. It was decided to ask the R. & A. at St Andrews for a ruling and in the meantime Sutherland and Macpherson played off again on the following day.

In the end of the day the first winner was [Dr] L.W. Macpherson of Baberton and Muswell Hill who went on to win the trophy three times by 1898 and thus took possession of it. Another handsome silver cup was commissioned from Mappin and Webb, the London silversmiths, and purchased for £39 :1 :5 and is played for to the present day. This cup is now valued at over £6000 and no longer is permitted to leave the club. After Dr Macpherson's death the original trophy was returned to the club and is now awarded to the winner of the low handicap section in the tournament.

The winner of the second championship in 1895 — decided by medal play over seventy-two holes — was [Dr] A.J.T. Allan of Watsonians who went on to win the British Amateur Championship at Muirfield in 1897. He died on 3rd March 1898 at the early age of twenty-two years and is today commemorated by the Jack Allan trophy which is presented to the winner of the Scottish Universities individual championship. Ten years later, in 1907, Harold Hilton wrote a newspaper article in which he referred to "the greatest golf ball incident in my experience" which occurred in Allan's match in the final of the British Amateur. At the time, Allan was a twenty-one year old medical student at Edinburgh University and he travelled daily to Muirfield by train and bicycle and played golf in his walking shoes. His opponent in the final was James Robb, a nineteen year-old student at St Andrews University. Going to the eleventh hole the caddies, as usual, went on in front to watch the flight and arrival of the balls over the hill. Both players hit their second shots and Allan's ball struck a stone wall well out of sight of many of the spectators. A search was made for the ball, as Allan would lose the hole if it could not be found. Eventually a well-known amateur asked Robb's caddie to turn out his pockets, and to the astonishment of the onlookers the missing ball was produced. The hole was given to Allan and Robb became three down and was beaten by four and two.

In Queen Victoria's Diamond Jubilee Year in 1897 the format of the Northern Amateur was again changed and the eight players with the lowest scratch scores over thirty-six holes medal play decided the winner by match play. The following year saw sixteen qualifiers for the first time and there was no further change until July 1950 when the Council unanimously decided to have thirty-two qualifiers in both the scratch and handicap sections.

J.Gordon Simpson of The Royal and Ancient golf club of St Andrews won the Northern in 1903 and later gained nine Scottish caps and played against the United States in the inaugural match in 1921 which preceded the Walker Cup.

Arguably the best golfer to win at Lossiemouth was the young Robert Harris of Carnoustie in 1904. Already a much travelled and experienced golfer, he was to appear in three British Amateur Championship finals, being beaten by Harold Hilton at St Andrews and Roger Wethered at Deal, but finally winning at Westward Ho! in 1925 by the margin of 13 up and 12 to play. He was beaten in the fifth round of the Amateur at Muirfield in 1926 by the American Amateur Champion Bobby Jones. Jones, in that year, travelling by sea on the *Aquitania,* became the first golfer to win both the British and American Open Championships, and in a period of seventeen days. Harris won twelve Scottish caps from 1905 and played three times against the Americans.

Two more Scottish internationals were the winners of the Northern Amateur in [Dr] F.H. Scroggie of Carnoustie in 1906 and Gordon Lockhart of Prestwick St Nicholas in 1907. Lockhart retained the title in 1908 beating that year's Cambridge captain V.C. Longstaffe (Aldeburgh) on his way to the final. After being a semi-finalist in the British Amateur of 1911 and winning the Irish Amateur Championship in 1912, Lockhart turned professional in 1921 and was appointed the first professional at Gleneagles. The secretary's report of the 1908 competition contained the information that the entrants included members of Royal Dornoch, Royal Aberdeen, Inverness, Nairn, Mid-Surrey, Royal Wimbledon, Deal, Tantallon, Muswell Hill, Princes, Mortonhall and many other golf clubs.

John Sutherland, the famous secretary of Royal Dornoch for more than fifty years, had figured prominently in the early years of the Northern Amateur at Lossiemouth, and another great publicist for Dornoch and fellow-member Donald Grant was the winner in 1909, beating Lieut. W.D. Allan of Moray who was the first Lossiemouth club member to reach the final. In his short book, *Personal Memories of Royal Dornoch Golf Club 1900-1925*, which has a foreword by Tom Watson and a preface by Herbert Warren Wind, Donald Grant relates the story of the Northern championship at Lossiemouth, 1909.

> Returned from Hamburg across the North Sea, to Firth of Forth, I cabled my entry at Lossiemouth for what was then called The Northern Championship. There were far fewer tournaments then. I stayed with an uncle on Findrassie Farm [Elgin], borrowed a bicycle for my five miles into Lossie each day, and picked up my own seven clubs at the pro's shop there. From my Northern Counties Cup play at Lossie in 1906, I had some knowledge of the golf course and I liked it. I felt I was playing for Dornoch as much as for myself. I duly qualified after two rounds medal play.
>
> Two more days of really keen match play followed: but first of all there was the sweepstake at five bob a head. "Old John Birnie", golfer and Provost of Inverness, drew my name in the sweepstake, more than happy to have a Dornoch golfer; he knew me personally, of course. I played good confident golf; to this day I remember some of my chip shots. My second and third round matches were the toughest. D.G. Mackenzie, plus 2, Mortonhall [golf club] Edinburgh, I met in the second round and got through; then I had to play a more notable golfer (and well I knew it), Gordon Lockhart, Troon, a Scots international golfer, who later became pro at Gleneagles. I managed to beat him, too, but it was a close match and I still remember it. The final was not so hard a match. I noticed, however, that I was pale and sort of haggard at the end of the three days of mounting concentration, as match followed keen match.

Donald Grant is well-known in America as the author of the personal story of Donald Ross, in the book entitled *Donald Ross of Pinehurst and Royal Dornoch — 1872-1948*.

The wealth of Dornoch talent at this time was epitomised by Charles E. Dick, whose home course was Royal Liverpool but who was also a member and frequent competitor at Dornoch. By 1907 he had appeared five times in the last eight of the British Amateur Championship and that year he won the St George's Challenge Cup of the Royal St George's club at Sandwich, joining a select band which was later to include Jack Nicklaus. In 1911, with five Scottish caps under his belt, he entered the Northern championship at Lossiemouth and beat the first-class Moray amateur George Thomson in the final. Thomson was often favourite to win on his own course, and in 1913 he became the first member of the club in twenty years to take the title. He appeared in the final again in 1921 but was beaten by G.C. Manford of Luffness New.

George Thomson

George Thomson was far and away the best amateur golfer produced by the Moray Golf Club in its first forty years. Born in 1890, he was to follow in his father's footsteps as a chemist in Elgin and always had to work for a living, unlike many of the golfers he encountered in his playing career. He showed early evidence of his talent by breaking the course record at the age of fifteen and winning the club championship at sixteen. He was club champion for six consecutive years and eleven times in all up to 1926, a record which endured for almost sixty years. At the age of sixteen, and playing off scratch, he entered his first Northern Amateur

George Thomson — the first Moray winner of the Northern Amateur Championship receives the trophy from Miss Asquith — 1913

and reached the semi-final. On the way to the final against C.E. Dick in the great year of 1911 he beat Colin C. Aylmer (Devon) who had been a finalist in the British Amateur the previous year. [Sir] Ernest Holderness (Walton Heath), an Oxford Blue who was twice to be British Amateur Champion, came down from Dornoch in 1911 but failed to qualify for the scratch sixteen. Thomson had an outstanding matchplay record and won the Spey Bay, Cruden Bay and Nairn tournaments while still in his teens, and competed in the British Amateur at Muirfield in 1909.

G.C. Manford of Edinburgh University won the Northern Amateur in 1914, the last championship for six years.

The Aftermath of War

The obverse of one of the two medals awarded to all those who served in the First World War proclaimed "The Great War For Civilisation 1914-19" and, in a speech at Wolverhampton, Lloyd George swiftly promised "to make Britain a fit country for heroes to live in". The Moray Golf Club in 1919 offered all Lossiemouth men who had fought in the war the opportunity for Privileged Membership. This was eagerly taken up and the schoolmaster John Hunter was appointed to look after and supervise the Privileged Members. The membership fee was fixed at ten shillings and sixpence, which was half the ordinary annual fee, and for this the ex-servicemen were allowed to play on the course after 6 o'clock in the evening, but they were not allowed to enter the clubhouse. At a later Council meeting it was unanimously agreed that after September 15th they could begin play after 5 o'clock. Some of them became very fine golfers and numbered among their members some of the fastest players, and straightest hitters of a golf ball, in the Moray Golf Club. At this distance in time the actions of the Council of the day suggest that they had little contact with the lives of ordinary people. They might well have been easing their consciences and keeping the locals quiet while the members of the club continued to enjoy social pre-eminence.

The long-standing friendly relationship with the Senior Service continued and officers of the fleet whose ships were at Invergordon or in the vicinity of Lossiemouth in the Moray Firth before and after World War One were made honorary members of the golf club during their stay so that they could play over the links. The club still possesses a handsome telescope given by the officers of the Second Cruiser Squadron in 1910, and also an aerial photograph of the course presented in gratitude by the officers of H.M.S. *Vindictive* in 1925.

The end of the First World War, and the inflationary years, posed other problems for the golf club. The price of whisky had to be increased to 6 pence a nip, and 1/- the glass from 3½ pence and 7 pence. Increased duty forced the Council to increase the price of claret to 2/- the pint, with port and sherry at 1/- the glass and brandy at 1/6 the glass. The price of the three course luncheon could not long be maintained at 2/6 and was increased to 3/-. It was also reported that there were no liqueurs in the clubhouse and that these were often asked for by members and visitors. The purchase was authorised of a suitable quantity of Benedictine, Kummel, Creme de Menthe, Vermouth and Liqueur Brandy from R.B. Smith & Son, Wine Merchants, Perth. Serious consideration was given whether or not to continue the telephone service in the clubhouse at an annual cost of £6 for 500 calls. A Council member recalled that in 1913 there had been practically no consumption of champagne and claret in stock at the clubhouse and it had been agreed that the captain take these over at the price standing in the books of the club amounting to £12 :0 :5.

The end of the war brought a flood of applications for membership. Among the many new members admitted to the club were C.C. Barrie, Esq. M.P., Airlie Park, Broughty Ferry, Sheriff D.J. Mackenzie, 17, Atholl Gardens, Glasgow, Sir Warren Fisher, H.M. Treasury, London, Lady Fisher, 31 Royal Avenue, Chelsea, Sir James Stewart-Lockhart, c/o the Hongkong & Shanghai Bank, Dalziel Hedderwick, 4, The Albany, Liverpool, Edwin Hedderwick, Barcelona, Major Frederick Forsyth, Cavalry Club, London, The Earl of Wilton, Warren Towers, Newmarket, and Sir Frederick Lobnitz of Ross Hall, Renfrewshire. The social revolution was a long away off.

The return to peace gave a fresh impetus to golf throughout the country and this was accompanied by numerous books on how to play the game. In 1920 Stancliffe recommended "On Driving — A steady, easy swing back, thinking all the time, and saying mentally God Save The King; this should take you to the top of the swing. Then when the downward stroke begins, think, BANG, quickly, and let the club act up to it, a sort of salute to the King. Of course you can say it aloud if you like, but not if your opponent objects, and says it puts him off."

The Northern tournament after the war was not held until 1920 when the first all-Moray final took place and Captain Kynoch Cumming won the cup from A.G. Campbell, beating [Dr] William Tweddell of Aberdeen University in the quarter finals. Dr Tweddell won the British Amateur of 1927 and later became captain of the Royal and Ancient, but he failed in repeated attempts to win at Lossiemouth.

G.C. Manford won his first cap for Scotland in 1922 and also his third Northern Amateur championship. In the final he beat another very good golfer in G. Seymour Noon of Didsbury golf club, Manchester. Noon went on to win nine Welsh caps and was runner-up in the Welsh Amateur Championships of 1934 and 1935. In 1923 W.C. White became the eighth Mortonhall player to appear in the Northern Amateur final in which he defeated T.H. Osgood of Forres and St Andrews, a future Cambridge Blue and Scottish International.

By this time the Scottish Golf Union had strongly recommended that the use of the word Championship should be dropped, the intention being to restrict its use to Scottish Amateur and Professional Championships. The annual competition thus became the Moray Open Amateur Tournament.

The Railway

In the summer of 1923 the railway had introduced a sleeping-car between London (Kings Cross) and Lossiemouth, via Aberdeen, to ease the passage of golfers and visitors to and from Lossiemouth. On arrival in Aberdeen from London the sleeping-car was attached to an express which left at 7.45 a.m. with the recently introduced breakfast-car attached. Elgin was reached via Craigellachie at 9.56 a.m., and Lossiemouth at 10.20 a.m.. Ian Peebles the cricketer — whose father was minister at Birnie Kirk in Moray — recalls, like many others, getting on the dining-car of the Elgin train in Aberdeen and breakfasting on fresh herrings done in oatmeal and accompanied by warm, fluffy baps.

The third Moray player to win in front of his home crowd was the Burghead schoolmaster A.G. Campbell in 1924. He accomplished the not inconsiderable feat of beating the reigning Scottish Amateur champion

Willis Mackenzie (Mortonhall) who had won his title earlier in the summer in the first national championship played at the Royal Aberdeen golf club. Mackenzie played in the first Walker Cup match in America in 1922 and he won the Scottish Amateur again in 1928. In 1925, Jack Bookless of Inverness and Moray beat J.G. Rowan (Drumpellier) for the Moray Amateur and went on to take the Scottish Amateur in 1929.

Local men began to figure more prominently in the competition around this time. J.L. Laing was runner-up in 1927, Hugo Ronald won it in 1930 and schoolmaster Alec McKenzie was runner-up in 1931. The winner in 1932 was Robert Falconer of Moray, and the Lossiemouth secondary school headmaster Dr J.C. Jessop had a hat trick of victories — 1934-36-39 — before the war.

Dr Jessop was a very fine golfer and keen student of the game — good enough to play in the Open Championship and write a popular instruction book called *Teach Yourself Golf*.

Dr Jessop's wins were interspersed with three successes by the colourful Aberdeen University golfer R.S. Walker. Dick Walker was a member of the Johnnie Walker whisky family and he matriculated at the University to study theology. He came to Aberdeen in 1934 via Winchester and Oxford, where he had been a triple Blue, and he soon became a member of an exceptional Aberdeen University golf team captained by W. Ferrier Mavor. Walker, a man of considerable strength, often lived in the summer in a caravan by the eighteenth hole of Cruden Bay golf course and was an assiduous practiser who was reputed to hit a thousand practice balls every day. He was instantly recognisable by his golfing garb, a dark grey fisherman's jersey worn with a pair of grey slacks, and the absence of socks. In hot weather he was attired in very short — for these days — shorts.

Dick Walker won five international caps for Scotland and a host of tournaments. In the British Amateur Championship at Hoylake in 1933 he lived in a tent on the beach and reached the quarter-finals before losing by two and one. In the finals he appeared in at Lossiemouth he beat a renowned competitor in Harvey Mackintosh of Royal Aberdeen — said by his friend Lewis Middleton to be the man who invented gamesmanship — and twice defeated a very fine golfer in Donald Cameron of Kirkintilloch and the Royal and Ancient. Cameron won many top class amateur events and after playing for Scotland he was twice non-playing captain and also a Walker Cup selector. The late Lewis Middleton was a past captain of Royal Aberdeen golf club and a noted golfer in the north-east of Scotland. In his humorous, tongue-in-cheek, contribution to the history of his golf club he had this to say of another past captain.

> Next I recall Harvey Mackintosh, the man who invented gamesmanship. On the tee he would jingle coins in his pocket, on the green he would move about, and between shots tell the most lurid stories, all designed to put his opponent off. Harvey was an awkward partner to play with in foursomes. Always extremely straight himself, if you drove into the rough he would go up and have a look at the lie which very often wasn't bad at all. Nonetheless with a look of disdain he would simply hit the ball sideways on to the fairway.

Post-war

After the Second World War the type of summer visitor changed. The post-war scarcity of motor cars, and the rationing of petrol, food, bread and spirits, with the lack of suitable accommodation, combined to keep away many, but not all, pre-war visitors and members. Who now remembers that rationing of bread in units was introduced in July 1947 and that two Bread Units equalled one small loaf of 14oz.? In December 1947 the golf club decided to increase the whisky ration on Christmas and New Year's Day to four small nips per person, and to remove the rationing of gin for the same days.

The young men of Lossiemouth and the surrounding district returning from the war began to figure more prominently in the membership and write their names in the golfing history of the club. The first Moray Open after the war was won by a local fisherman, George T. Murray, in 1946. This was a signal of the social revolution which was about to change the Moray Golf Club irrevocably. At long last it became a golf club for local people. Fishermen, who for so long had largely been denied entry, joined in large numbers.

W.D. Campbell, the banker, scored the first of his two victories in 1948, and the beaten finalist Walter Wilken is still playing consistently to a handicap of six at Elgin golf club some forty years later. Dr Jessop chalked up his fourth and last win in 1949, fifteen years after he won his first Moray Open.

B.W. Wilken congratulates W.D. Campbell on winning the Moray Open — 1948

Dr Horace Thomson of Elgin in 1951 came within a whisker of emulating his father's success in 1913. He lost on the seventeenth green in an exciting match to W.D. Campbell, whose brilliant iron play was a feature of the game. The runner-up next year was a regular visitor to Lossiemouth, James Lindsay of Falkirk Tryst — later to be President of the Scottish Golf Union. He was already a distinguished golfer, having won the British Boys Amateur Championship in the years 1929 and 1930, and he was the possessor of nine pre-war Scottish caps. He went one better in 1953 when he beat Ian Rodger — now the professional at Elgin golf club — in the final. Ian Rodger was the first man to win the Elgin and Moray club championships and the Open amateur tournaments of both golf clubs, a considerable feat which has since been equalled by Norman Grant, the most consistently successful golfer in Moray who has often been watched by the Scottish selectors.

Chris MacLeod

The first of a number of home-bred young lions emerged in 1954 when Christopher MacLeod, an eighteen year-old Elgin Academy schoolboy, defeated nineteen year-old Farquhar Thomson, also of the Moray Golf Club, in the semi-finals of the Moray Open. In the final, MacLeod far outdrove his opponent D.F. Beatson of Kingsnowe, Edinburgh, but MacLeod's deplorable putting — he three-putted the eleventh, twelfth, thirteenth and sixteenth holes — assured him of defeat by three and two. However, in 1955 he won the Elgin Open amateur tournament, defeating James Lindsay in the final, and repeated the performance on a return visit to the area in 1965 when he beat the experienced R.M. (Chanto) Grant.

Chris MacLeod driving at the thirteenth hole — 1988

MacLeod was Scottish Universities champion in 1958 — winning the trophy in memory of Dr Jack Allan who had won the Moray Open at Lossiemouth in the nineteenth century — and the following year he began to demonstrate his great ability. Always very long off the tee, he now had a very efficient short game to match and he was soon amongst the trophies. The first was the Moray county championship at Grantown-on-Spey which he won by a record sixteen strokes with rounds of sixty-six and sixty-eight, in spite of a two stroke penalty in his first round when he played his partner's ball. Then followed the one-day Open at Lossiemouth and with rounds of seventy-four and seventy-two he scored another runaway victory by eight strokes from Ian Rodger.

MacLeod followed that up with a comprehensive defeat of Simon Smith in the final to win the Moray Open for the first time, and with his confidence high, set off for St Andrews and the Scottish Amateur Championship. In the first round he met and defeated Stuart Murray (Elderslie) who had already played for Great Britain, and reached the fifth round before departing. Another north player, R.D. Gordon of Nairn, also acquitted himself well by knocking out the holder W.D. Smith (Selkirk) and reaching the sixth round. This led *The Northern Scot* reporter to express the pious, and wildly optimistic, hope that the Scottish selectors would no doubt show more respect for players in this area.

Chris MacLeod won the Nairn Open in 1960 and the Moray Open again in 1961, beating a formidable competitor in R.M. (Chanto) Grant, of the Caledonian golf club in Aberdeen, with a birdie three at the third extra hole. He soon was lost to golf at Lossiemouth when he joined the R.A.F., in which he reached the rank of Squadron Leader, and he won the R.A.F. championship at his first attempt. He marked his return from the service at the age of forty-five in 1981 by again reaching the final of the Moray Open, being defeated by his clubmate Michael Wilson. In 1984, thirty years after his first appearance in the final, he once more reached the last stage but had to give best to Jim Scott of Murcar and Royal Dornoch. A very able committee member, MacLeod induced the Council to buy a computer and himself wrote the handicapping programme which is still in use and which he updates regularly.

S.L. McKinlay, writing in the October 1960 edition of *Golfing*, had this to say of MacLeod at his best.

Chris MacLeod is less well known to Scottish golfers, largely because he plays most of his golf in the North, but he is a very fine player who might easily become a great one if he lived and worked and played in a sternly competitive milieu. He is a school teacher and spends his summer vacation playing in the tournaments at the holiday resorts along the Moray Firth, which usually attract some tidy players from distant parts. This summer he won four in a row including the Nairn competition of which I count myself fortunate to have seen the closing stages.

In the final he met an Inland Revenue official, James McBeath, who had a very proper regard for economy in figures as befitted his profession, and was five under fours when he holed out on the seventeenth — and had the grace to give warm congratulations to his conqueror. MacLeod, as my sceptical eyes can testify, was a genuine seven under fours for seventeen holes on the fine testing Nairn course [and] he was as near perfection as I have ever seen any golfer approach. I hope I'll see a lot of golf in the years to come; I cannot hope to see better figures more easily fashioned.

Add to this accomplishment of MacLeod's that he is well-made, athletic, and as handsome as Dirk Bogarde, whom he strongly resembles, and you can imagine how the gallery gurgled.

Farquhar Thomson had been knocking on the door for some time and landed the Moray Open in 1962 in the first of his three final appearances. In 1964, when he was club champion, he lost in the final to Bill Reid, the genial butcher from Hopeman, near Lossiemouth. Bill Reid had been a member at Moray for two years and this was his second attempt at the Open. He was a late starter, having taken up golf when he was almost thirty years of age, but he had already won the Elgin Open three times and the Elgin club championship on five occasions. Thomson appeared in the final again in 1969 and lost to Norman Grant by two and one.

Alistair Thomson

Farquhar Thomson's younger brother Alistair — professional to the Moray Golf Club for the past eleven years — lived in Farquhar's shadow for some years, but Alistair won the Moray Open in 1966 on the eighteenth green after a great battle with Ian Rodger who had opened with two threes. The following year the two met again in the final of the Elgin Open amateur and Rodger again opened with two threes and again lost at the eighteenth hole. Alistair Thomson was to win the Moray Open twice more, extracting the maximum of excitement from each occasion. He was a fearless match

Alistair Thomson — Professional to the Moray Golf Club — 1988

81

player who enjoyed single combat, and with his Palmer-like swing he was electrifying to watch and kept the galleries on their toes. In 1970 against Alistair P. Thomson — now professional at Inverness — with three birdies he was four up after five holes but lost the short sixth where his opponent had his first hole in one. The Lossiemouth Thomson went on to win by three and two.

Alistair Thomson's third and last victory was over Norman Grant in 1974 in a match of old rivalries and some tension. The eighteenth hole — David Hamilton has called it "surely the noblest finishing hole in Scotland" — highlighted the affair. Both hit long drives with Thomson, who was one hole up, in a deep bunker down the left of the fairway. Grant played a beautiful second to the long plateau green and lay some twelve feet away. Thomson played one of his famous recovery shots and lay outside his opponent. He proceeded to hole a bold putt for a birdie three and win one of the more exciting finals.

Norman Grant

The golfer without peer in the history of the last twenty-five years of the Moray Golf Club is undoubtedly senior local government officer Norman S. Grant of Lossiemouth. A member of both the Moray and Elgin golf clubs, he learned to play his golf at Elgin and his allegiance naturally lay there for many years, but the championship boards in the Moray clubhouse bear witness to his outstanding record as a seaside links player. A great competitor without any weaknesses in his game, since 1965 he

Norman Grant with the Moray Open trophy — 1967

has appeared in the final of the annual Moray tournament on no less than ten occasions and has been the winner of the trophy five times. He also enjoys the dubious distinction of having been beaten in the 1983 final by A.D. Nichols of Eaton, the first Englishman (albeit a county golfer) to win the title since it was first competed for so long ago in 1894. Grant's record in the club championship is even more impressive and he has won it fourteen times since 1966. His twelfth victory in 1985 eclipsed George Thomson's record which had stood for sixty years, although these two golfers of widely differing generations have each won the club championship six years in succession and remain tied on that score.

An automatic choice for the north district team for twenty-six years, Grant has met and beaten numerous Scottish internationals, and his failure to win a cap can only be ascribed to his geographical location. A cheerful and gregarious man, he has successfully applied his great energy and organising ability in recent years to the task of convener of entertainments on the Council, and with his ally George Reid has raised a large amount of money for the golf club.

Other Notables

When H.B. Stuart's work took him to live in Elgin he became a member at Moray and won the Open amateur in 1977 and 1978 when he was already a very distinguished golfer. Winner of the Scottish Boys' Championship in 1959 when a pupil at Forres Academy, he was Scottish Amateur Champion in 1972 and won a considerable number of caps both for Scotland and Great Britain. He played in three successive Walker Cup matches and acquitted himself with great distinction on the first occasion in 1971 at St Andrews when he won all his games.

The 1979 and 1988 Moray Opens were won by a well-known local man who is a banker in Banff, inter-district golfer Ian McIntosh. A very experienced competitor with a slow and graceful swing who hits the ball a long way, Ian McIntosh has won his fair share of bets and tournaments.

Ian McIntosh with Ben Crenshaw at Royal Dornoch

In 1988, as organiser and group leader, he bravely and cheerfully led a cohort of Moray Golf Club members of all ages on a very successful golfing holiday to Portugal, and it is hoped, if he can spare the time from his work, and the otiose support of a Glasgow football club, that this will become an annual event. In winning the 1988 Moray Open he played some golf of rare quality, not least in the quarter-final when, on the eighteenth green, he defeated an old adversary in Norman Grant who holed the course in sixty-nine, one shot more than McIntosh. In 1988 he also won the thirty-six hole Tantalus over the Moray course beating Scottish international Keith Hird, a frequent competitor at Lossiemouth, by one stroke.

Norman Grant won his last Moray Open in 1980 when he met and defeated a fine golfing greenkeeper, Michael Wilson of Moray. Wilson appeared in the final on three successive occasions winning the last two in 1981 and 1982, and capturing the Nairn Open in addition. A phlegmatic personality with a rather droll sense of humour, Wilson was frequently to be seen to turn off his hearing aid from tee to green which effectively isolated him from the noise of spectators and passing aircraft.

The Moray Open in recent years has attracted very large fields now that both eighteen-hole courses are used for the qualifying rounds, and the consolation rounds are played on the New course while the match play stages are decided over the Old course. This innovation, largely due to the present captain Farquhar Thomson, has led to fields of almost three hundred competitors, and once more golfers from further afield are appearing in the final stages. A welcome sight is the reappearance of low handicap golfers from Aberdeen and the south and it is a pleasure to record that since 1982 all the winners bar one have been from other clubs. The tournament has been sponsored by individuals and firms since 1977 and a unique feature of the qualifying rounds is that each one of the thirty-six holes carries prizes in the form of golf balls or vouchers for birdies or eagles, and at some holes, the longest drives or the lowest aggregates for the short holes.

CHAPTER VIII

The Ladies

WOMEN have always played a prominent part in the history of the Moray Golf Club. They embraced the game of golf from the outset with the same enthusiasm as men, and until recent years, comprised more than a third of the membership. In the days between the wars their number has been difficult to quantify because of the very large number of temporary members or visitors. The peak was probably reached in 1928 — out of a total of 832 annual members no fewer than 319 were women and the great majority were playing members. In that year the income from visitors almost exactly equalled the income from annual subscriptions, a state of affairs which has not again been approached.

Centenary year will see the fourth time the Scottish Ladies' Amateur Championship will have been held at Lossiemouth. This is a well-deserved tribute to a fine championship course and to the achievements of Moray women golfers through the years. The Scottish Ladies' was first played at Lossiemouth in 1912 and Miss Dorothy M. Jenkins beat Miss M. Neil Fraser by 4 and 2 in the final.

The Championship returned to Lossiemouth in 1923 and a prominent member of the Moray Golf Club in Mrs W.H. Nicolson of Murrayfield, beat Mrs J.B. Watson (Murrayfield) by 2 and 1 in the final. Mrs Watson (later Mrs Charlotte Beddows) had won the title for the three previous years, and on the way to the final she beat the Lossiemouth girl Ena Fraser at the 20th hole in an exciting semi-final. Mrs Nicolson was Ladies' champion of the Moray Golf Club in 1920, 1922 and again in 1923.

Miss Mary Benton was a very prominent golfer in the early days of the club and she was succeeded by a series of fine young golfers. She was Ladies' champion six times between 1906 and 1919 and was still playing off a handicap of four in 1936.

Hilda Cameron

Hilda Cameron and Kathleen Macdonald were pupils of that noted Lossiemouth teaching professional George Smith and quickly made their mark at local, national and international level from 1923 onwards. There was very little to choose between them and both were outstanding golfers. Hilda Cameron had an excellent record in the Scottish Ladies' Amateur Championship. She was beaten in the final at Turnberry in 1924, in the semi-final at Cruden Bay in 1926 and again in the final at Machrihanish in 1927. The golf correspondent of *The Glasgow Herald* wrote of the 1927 final:

85

Miss Inglis and Miss Cameron, having survived the longest, necessarily impressed most, and it was indeed very impressive golf they played, so uniformly good that the issue was in the balance all the way, even when the balls lay two yards from the hole on the eighteenth green. It was a fine performance [by Miss Inglis] to win at the third time of trying. Yet Miss Cameron's record is very impressive, with two silver medals and one bronze out of four Championships. Success must come to her too, very soon.

The Scotsman expressed similar sentiments.

In the quarter-finals of the British Ladies' Amateur Championship of 1930 at Formby, Hilda lost by one hole to the great American champion Glenna Collett in what was to be Miss Collett's second successive appearance in the final. Hilda Cameron played for Scotland in all the international matches of 1927, 1928, 1929 and 1931 and she was club champion on six occasions between 1926 and 1933. She won the Northern counties championship three times in succession from 1930 and as Mrs A.A. Marr she brought further honour to the Moray club as runner-up in 1935 and winner in 1936 of the All-India Ladies' Championship. This championship was always held at the Royal Calcutta Golf Club at Tollygunge — one of the oldest golf clubs in the world outside Britain.

Kathleen Macdonald

Kathleen Macdonald was another distinguished representative of the Moray Golf Club in a sadly brief golfing career. In 1926 at the age of 19 she and Hilda Cameron lost in the semi-finals to the eventual winners of the Eves' foursomes which used to precede the Scottish Ladies' Amateur Championship. The following year she made her mark by beating a field of 70, including two ex-Scottish champions, in an open medal competition in a gale of wind over the No. 1 course at Gullane.

Kathleen Macdonald

In May 1928 in the British Ladies' Championship at Hunstanton she was beaten at the eighteenth hole in the third round by clubmate Hilda Cameron who herself succumbed in the following round. As the youngest Scottish cap at Hunstanton Kathleen won all her matches against Ireland, England and Wales by the decisive margins of 2 up, 6 and 5 and 5 and 4.

In June she entered the Scottish Ladies' Championship at St Andrews and lost to three times former champion Mrs J.B. Watson (later Mrs Charlotte Beddows) of Murrayfield in the third round. In what was described as "the match of the round" in front of a large gallery, Mrs Watson put an immense putt to the lip of the sixteenth to halve it in 4, holed a five yarder for a desperate half at the seventeenth, and finally ran down one almost double that length to win the eighteenth and the match. So wrote international golfer Miss Eleanor Helme of *The Morning Post,* fellow member at Moray and champion there in 1914. *The Daily Mail* and the *Evening Times* were no less flattering.

Less attention was paid to another very fine golfer from Moray who was also tutored by George Smith. Peggy Ramsay was a member of a Scottish family who lived in Alnmouth, Northumberland, and spent their summers in Lossiemouth where her father had built a substantial house, "Hillhead" in Dunbar Street, as a holiday home. She worked her way quietly through the top half of the draw and was beaten 2 and 1 in the final by Jean McCulloch of West Kilbride. This was no surprise as Miss Ramsay had already been twice in the final of the Northumberland Ladies' championship and reached the final again in 1928.

Hilda Cameron, playing really well and looking for that elusive first title, unfortunately sprained her ankle the week before the championship and lost in the first round to Mrs J.A. Cruickshank of Troon who, as Dorothy Jenkins, won the Scottish at Lossiemouth in 1912.

Four times in six years and twice in succession the Moray Golf Club had produced a finalist. Surely it was only a matter of time before the Scottish title returned to Lossiemouth. In 1929 Kathleen Macdonald was beaten in the third round of both the British and the Scottish but in the latter she had the satisfaction of knocking out the holder Jean McCulloch. 1930 was a great year for the Moray girls at Formby in the British Ladies' Amateur. With an excellent field of 180 including a large American contingent, Hilda Cameron and Kathleen Macdonald were the only Scots to reach the last eight. Kathleen defeated a redoubtable American, Virginia van Wie, (the winner of the American Ladies' Amateur Championship three times in succession from 1932), on her way to the semi-final, where she lost to the eventual winner of the championship, Diana Fishwick — later Mrs A.C. Critchley.

In 1932, at the age of 25, Kathleen Macdonald won the All-India Ladies' Championship at Calcutta and died at Colombo soon afterwards. Today the ladies play the K.S.M. foursomes in her memory.

Meg Farquhar Main

Meg Farquhar Main became assistant professional to the late George Smith at Lossiemouth at the age of 19 in 1929. She became the fourth assistant of that incomparable teacher, the other three being Willie Crockett, John Campbell and Dennis Christie. Willie Crockett soon took up a post in America and W.S. MacDonald was appointed assistant in his place. It was a sign of the prosperity of the Moray Golf Club that the professional could employ four assistants throughout the years of the depression.

It seems likely that Meg Farquhar, as she was then, was the first female assistant professional in British golf, although Poppy Wingate in England soon after became assistant to her brother Syd at Temple Newsam, Leeds. Meg Farquhar learned all the skills of clubmaking, finishing and repairing, and became an accomplished teacher in her own right. She was the first woman to enter and compete on equal terms in a men's national championship when she played in the Scottish Professional Championship of 1933 at Lossiemouth. With rounds of 79 - 86 - 85 - 81, on a long testing seaside links with greens like lightning, she acquitted herself well and finished ahead of a surprising number of her male counterparts. The first

Meg Farquhar, Scottish Professional Championship — 1933

woman professional to compete in a national Open Championship outside Britain was Genevieve le Derff who played in the French Open in 1929.

Although steel shafts had been legal in Britain since 1929 and conferred a distinct advantage, Meg Farquhar played throughout with her set of hickory-shafted irons. As a result of the prominence given to this she was invited to the British firm of Accles & Pollock Ltd. — who with an American company had formed the True Temper Corporation — and presented with a set of steel shafts which were made up by Nicoll of Leven. This was a fine consolation prize for a gallant performance.

Meg (Farquhar) Main was reinstated as an amateur in 1949 and quickly made her mark in Scottish golf by reaching the semi-final of the Scottish Ladies' at Troon that year, when she was beaten by the eventual winner Jean Donald who turned professional in 1953. This was her best effort in the Scottish although she reached the quarter-finals on a number of occasions subsequently. She played in the home internationals of 1950 at Newcastle, Co. Down, travelling over with fellow Moray member Chrystal MacGeagh who was in the Irish team. She won all her matches, and in the Irish match was drawn against Chrystal whom she beat comprehensively by 5 and 4. This encounter was to be repeated on the links at Stotfield on many occasions with Meg (just) having the better of the exchanges.

She was again selected for Scotland in 1951 and again rewarded the selectors by winning all her matches at Broadstone in Dorset. Such are the vagaries of the selection process that she never again was asked to play for Scotland although her golf was of such a high standard that she was still playing off plus one in 1957. Meg Main was Ladies' champion at Moray nine times between 1949 and 1969 and won the Northern counties championship on five occasions. She still lives in Lossiemouth and takes a great interest in her golf club of which she has the unusual distinction of being the sole honorary member.

On the last occasion the Scottish Ladies' Amateur was played at Lossiemouth in 1935, Miss M. Robertson Durham beat Miss Nan Baird at the 20th hole.

Chrystal MacGeagh

A prominent member of the club for many years and a most determined match player, Chrystal MacGeagh won the Irish Ladies' Championship at Bundoran in 1939 having been a semi-finalist in 1937 and reaching the semi-finals again in 1954. Apart from the war years she was an Irish international from 1938 to 1950 and played lacrosse for Ireland from 1930 to 1939.

Five times Ladies' champion at Moray, she competed frequently and successfully in men's competitions, winning the Silver Jubilee cup in 1950. She also won the low handicap section of the Moray Open tournament in 1949, a remarkable feat which has not so far been repeated. Meg Main made a brave attempt to emulate her in 1950 but finished as runner-up.

In 1930 the ladies made an application to the Council that they should pay the full subscription of two guineas and be granted the power to vote at the club's annual general meetings. This was firmly and unanimously turned down and it was many moons and repeated rebuffs before the granting of universal suffrage on 20th March 1959. The activities of Chrystal MacGeagh and Meg Main in playing in and winning men's competitions probably did little to further the ladies' cause.

Chrystal MacGeagh with the Irish Ladies' Championship Cup — 1939

The period after the second war was dominated by golfers of the calibre of Mrs K. Christie, Barbara Chetham, Margaret Cameron, Chrystal MacGeagh, Meg Main, Mrs Miller-Stirling, Mrs B. Spence — and the evergreen Mrs Hilda Marr, off a handicap of four, twenty years after her last appearance in the final of the Scottish Ladies'. Mrs Spence's husband — the late H.R. Spence of Huntly, member of Parliament and the Moray Golf Club — is remembered by older members of the club for driving the eighteenth green on a number of occasions when the course was baked hard in the summer time.

Mrs Iris Douglas, Mrs Wadham, Mrs Molly Scoular Buchanan, Mrs West, Miss Alice Anderson, Miss Jean Alexander and Mrs Markes all graced the silver division for many years, and Miss Ina Allan, Miss Ann Paterson and Mrs Elizabeth Saul were robust competitors in the bronze. Indeed Miss Allan continued to drive her Mini and to play golf until she was almost ninety, but now in her ninety-fifth year she confines her sporting activities to frequent games of bridge with her golfing friends. The most impressive ladies' club record in recent years belongs to Mrs Liz Munro (née Geddes) who has been champion thirteen times in seventeen years up to 1987.

The halcyon days for the ladies are gone, but the club can look back with pride to a time when they could boast of at least eight internationals and two national champions.

90

Chapter IX

The Professionals

IN July 1890 the Council engaged the thirty year-old Andrew Kirkaldy, the St Andrews professional, — who had also been advising on the work and layout of the course — as the teaching professional at Lossiemouth for the months of July and August, but at the last moment his mother's illness prevented him taking up the post. However, Tom Morris was able to arrange for David Cuthbert, also a well-known St Andrews professional, to fill the vacancy, and he proved very satisfactory, even to the extent of playing and winning all his matches against other clubs at the top of the Moray team. At the time of the caddies' strike against the sum of threepence a round in August of 1892, John Donald, the greenkeeper, was said to be a capital clubmaker for the members. The caddies did not publicise their strike for fear of dismissal but refused to carry the clubs of more than one visitor on the

Andrew Kirkaldy in old age

grounds that "he's ane o' the threepenny mans". A London newspaper-man reported that he was commonly asked "foo much?" and found that an acceptable fee was fourpence or even sixpence.

The first full-time professional attached to the club was David Brown in 1894, but apart from the fact that he came from Kinghorn in Fife, little is known about him. He played a number of matches for side bets against scratch amateur golfers and he defeated W.F. Orr of the Aberdeen club over four rounds at Lossiemouth. He won at the seventy-second hole as Orr was seen to improve his lie by moving his ball into a better position off his drive and Brown claimed the hole. Robert Stronnar followed Brown as professional and he supervised the considerable lengthening of the course in 1897 on the lines recommended by himself and Archie Simpson, the Aberdeen professional. The extended course was opened for play on 1st January 1898, but Stronnar resigned in November 1898 and Robert Scott of Carnoustie was appointed clubhouse-keeper and professional in his stead, from January 1899.

Scott was to keep the clubhouse and surrounds in a clean and tidy condition and serve spirits, beer and aerated waters which were the property of the club. He was also to provide luncheons and teas at prices fixed by the Council — and any profits from this source went to him. His duties involved superintending the workmen on the course — but taking all his instructions from the club officials — and its condition was his responsibility entirely. In addition he was to superintend, engage and pay caddies for members, and teach the game to members at a fee fixed by the Council. At the next meeting of the Council it was decided to allow Scott five pence per hour for his labour on the course as arranged with the green committee.

However, he had free fire and light and accommodation of a kitchen and two bedrooms in the clubhouse — although the Council reserved the right to a limited use of one of the bedrooms for lady players. (This was in the first clubhouse erected in 1892, which did not have a ladies' room, and presumably the bedroom was used as a changing room by the ladies). His salary was £30 a year payable quarterly, with commission of 15% on tickets sold to visitors. He was paid a fee of one penny per round for every caddie engaged, and a fee of 2/6 per round from members of the club for teaching, but he had to supply his own caddie. He was to sell and repair clubs in his workshop and sell golf balls for profit — otherwise his time was his own. Little wonder that Scott and his wife failed to stay the course and he was given notice twelve months later.

In January 1900 it was decided to divide the duties, and a member of the Council of the golf club, Alexander Hay of Seaholme, was appointed clubhouse-keeper and caddie-master with an allowance of £10 per annum. He was forbidden to sell clubs, balls etc., or to make repairs on his own account and he was not allowed to teach the game. Hay filled the post to everyone's satisfaction, and when he died in 1910 his wife became club-mistress until her death in 1918.

Charles Neaves (1871-1947) of the Bogside golf club, Irvine, had intimated that he was open for engagement and he was invited to become clubmaker and professional to the Moray Golf Club from April 1900. He was a native of Leven in Fife, where he learnt the game and began in the traditional way as a clubmaker. After a year or two in St Andrews he returned to Leven where he opened a clubmaker's shop and was known to the Thistle golf club members as a strong professional and a maker of good clubs.

This was the start of a long and fruitful relationship with the Moray Golf Club in which Charlie Neaves, as superintendent of the green staff, presided over many important changes on the Stotfield links. Many holes in the outward half particularly were lengthened — for example the fifth green was carried over the ridge to the natural hollow behind it — and the new nine-hole Relief course was constructed and opened in July 1906. Neaves' talents were widely recognised and in 1903 he was asked to lay out a golf course at Glenfeshie for Colonel Cooper and at Findhorn for the Findhorn Bay Hotel. Later he was to advise on improvements to the course at Fochabers.

Neaves was a fine golfer and played in many exhibition matches with the leading professionals of the day at Lossiemouth. He played several matches with his friends Joseph Dalgleish, the Nairn professional, and Archie Simpson of the Aberdeen club, both like himself from Fife, and both well-known clubmakers. Archie Simpson was perhaps the best golfer of the three having twice been runner-up in the Open Championship. Neaves competed in the Open more than once without success, and was capped for Scotland against Ireland at Portrush in 1907. His contacts undoubtedly played a part in attracting J.H. Taylor, Sandy Herd and James Braid to play over the Moray links. One who served his time as a clubmaker with Neaves was Alec Marling of Lossiemouth who won the Scottish Professional Championship of 1913 at Cruden Bay when it was played over three rounds, due to thick fog on the first day. Marling went to Forres golf club as professional, then to the Erskine club, Glasgow, and later to the Deeside golf club in Aberdeen for three years, before becoming the first of the Lossiemouth assistants to be appointed professional, and greenkeeper, at Royal Aberdeen when Archie Simpson went to America in 1912.

Numerous other assistants learned the art of club making with Charlie Neaves, and gave lessons to the golfers who flocked to the links at Stotfield. Eric Edwards and James Balfour of Lossiemouth were among them, but the latter died in 1923 at the early age of thirty-four. However, one of Neaves' assistants who was to become professional to the Moray Golf Club was the young James Mackenzie from Alness in Ross-shire who served in the First World War and later resumed his apprenticeship with George Smith. A number of fine examples of scared-neck wooden clubs made by Neaves still exist.

Neaves gave devoted service to his club both as professional and greenkeeper until the First World War and seemed to weather such storms as arose with equanimity. One such episode involved David West at a Council meeting on 17th July 1905. He moved "that Neaves be prohibited from drinking in the clubhouse and that, as he has failed to keep the hours fixed by the Council, his wages be reduced by £10". The motion was not seconded and was withdrawn by West. At the beginning of 1917 Neaves wrote the Council to say that he intended to go into the fishing industry, and was having a boat built for the purpose, and requested the Council to relieve him of his duties for the duration of the war. He had been having a thin time financially during the war years, and matters were not improved by David West's continual sniping. The last straw was West's allegation that Neaves had left the club by motor car on February 15th and spent the day curling.

The war appeared to be responsible for a fall in standards in other departments and the house committee were perturbed by complaints that the maids in the clubhouse frequently appeared, while attending on members, without caps or even aprons. As Neaves' income from the golf club fell he became more preoccupied with the construction of his fishing boat, and the secretary was instructed to write him and point out that the wartime arrangements were not proving satisfactory. A dignified reply, incorporating some pent-up feelings, was read to the next Council meeting.

> I have fully considered your letter to me of the 21st June and as you seem dissatisfied with the present arrangements I am left with no alternative but to sever my connection with the Club. My position has not been an enviable one for the last three years, not to say anything about the years before the War. All these petty

complaints against me have emanated from the same quarter of which I have absolute proof, and I am surprised the Council did not put a stop to it long ago. That man is the only member I have had words with during my long connection with the Club. My salary along with sales etc. has been quite inadequate during the last three years to keep me, and I certainly had to look about for something else to do, which was the Council's wish. I have tried to do my duty to the Club so far as lay in my power and I would like to leave the Club in the same manner as I have always tried to be, a gentleman.

His subsequent career was rather chequered. Like so many fishermen before and since, the fishing industry did not fulfil Neaves' expectations and he settled down ashore to the life of a general merchant and sub-postmaster in a small store — which serves the same function today — in the main street of Lossiemouth. He had also acquired by his efforts a large Edwardian villa in James Street which he proceeded to lose in an all-night card game to MacBeth the butcher. The citizens of Lossiemouth yield to no one in their admiration for a good golfer, but Charlie Neaves' recklessness in gambling away the substantial roof over his head is still talked of today in Lossiemouth in hushed tones.

Little did the club realise what a great teacher and fine golfer they were about to appoint when they asked a local man, George E. Smith, to help them out in 1917. He was to be the club professional for thirty-three years and his famed stable of assistants found professional posts all over the world. George won the Scottish Professional Championship of 1922 at Gleneagles, and played for Scotland against Ireland in 1932, but he was best known for his abilities as a teacher and golf clubmaker. From 1919 until the outbreak of the Second War in 1939 his professional's shop was a hive of industry, particularly during the close season. Rough turned persimmon blocks and hickory shafts came from America and were fashioned into wooden clubs — it is said that one could tell which assistant had made the club by the shape of the head. Beech was used as well as persimmon as it was cheaper, and each club was made to suit the customer. The finished head was produced with rasp, file, and sand paper and then stained and hand-polished with shellac and linseed oil. Iron heads were purchased and made up with hickory shafts and finished. Willie MacDonald, one of the assistant professionals, recalls that, working flat out, he could make six clubs in a day, and on occasion during the summertime he worked until eleven o'clock at night at repairing members' clubs for the next day.

In 1927 George Smith was advertising in a local newspaper that he had a stock of nearly a thousand hand-made clubs to choose from at a price ranging from seven shillings and sixpence to twenty-one shillings. He also advertised the Moray golf ball at one shilling and sixpence and the Lossie golf ball at one shilling and threepence, with the added incentive of "fourpence to eightpence allowed for old balls in exchange for either of the above balls". It would be interesting to know how the "ball hawks" of 1927 dealt with that threat to their livelihood. Although the Moray Golf Club is a private club, the land on which the two eighteen-hole courses are laid out is leased from the proprietors and is unfenced. The public, at their own risk, have always been able to walk freely on the land and a number of men, who are not members, spend their time searching for, and finding, lost golf balls. They are commonly referred to by the members as "ball hawks" and are not popular.

George E. Smith, Professional 1917-1950

95

From the early 1920's until 1939 there were never fewer than four assistant professionals at Lossiemouth and often six, although one was a lady shop assistant in the summer months. John Grant, who became professional at Boat of Garten, and Willie Cattell who went to America, were amongst the early assistants. In the 1920's the assistants were Willie Crockett, Willie Souter, John Campbell and Dennis Christie and after Souter had gone to America, George Smith gave the 19 year-old Meg Farquhar the opportunity to become the first woman assistant professional in 1929. Crockett soon departed for America and W.S. MacDonald was recruited to fill the vacancy. Willie Souter (Bill in America) became assistant to George Smith at the age of fifteen in 1921. At the end of his five year apprenticeship he emigrated to the New World and found a post at Jacksonville Golf and Country club in Florida alongside Willie Cattell. He remained there until the war in which he served with the American paratroopers. He then became professional at Whispering Pines before moving to nearby Green Valley golf club, Greensboro, as assistant teaching professional. Gordon Wilken of Elgin, who later became the very efficient secretary of the Elgin golf club, was an assistant at Lossiemouth for two years, as was Hamish Harthill who lost his life as an R.A.F. pilot in the Second War.

The clubmaking continued apace and Smith decided to break new ground by applying for six months leave of absence from 1st October 1933. This was granted and the intrepid Smith set sail for Hong Kong and Japan to sell his golf clubs and teach the locals to play golf. George Smith laid great emphasis on the swing in teaching, and there is a story of how, many years later, one of the overseas members of the Moray Golf Club came across a Chinaman in Hong Kong with a set of George Smith clubs. When he remarked on this he was greeted with the cheerful reply — "Ah yes, swingee swingee — swingee swingee." This was the first of two sorties by Smith to the Far East, and he later visited the Chinese mainland and broke the course record at Canton with a score of thirty-three for its nine-hole course, and recorded his first ever hole in one there.

George Smith loved to tell jokes and stories about golf and golfers. One of his favourites was of playing with friends in a fourball when they noticed a player ahead of them behaving in a strange fashion. He continually kicked or threw his ball into bunkers or gorse or deep into the rough and then attempted to play it out. Finally curiosity overcame them and they asked the man what he was doing. "Oh", came the reply, "I'm getting in some practice for the club mixed foursomes on Saturday."

George Smith's deafness was due to one of two wounds received when serving with the 4th Battalion of the Gordon Highlanders in the First World War. He spoke with a loud, cheerful and penetrating voice which on occasion caused problems for his friends. In 1953 the author and his wife made the journey to Carnoustie to see the one visit of the legendary Ben Hogan to our Open Championship. Hogan had arrived two weeks beforehand to familiarise himself with a long and difficult seaside links and in the end won comfortably. Smith had gone down the previous day to see some friends and we finally caught up with Hogan and his partner at the seventeenth hole of the third round. We saw George at the moment he saw us, and standing on a knoll by the green he called loudly to us over the startled gallery "Hallo — Hogan was in the bunker and he's about to take six." Hogan duly obliged and we slunk off with our collars turned up.

George Smith and Alec Marling had a sports shop near the railway station in Aberdeen for a time and later George had another sports shop in Batchen Street in Elgin as well as a newsagents business in Lossiemouth which was managed by his brother Hugh. He wrote a number of articles for *The Elgin Courant* on how to improve your golf and these were later published in book form as *Hints to Golfers.* Many well-known golfers came to him to have their swings straightened out and he gave golf lessons to Prince Philip — The Duke of Edinburgh — when he was at Gordonstoun before the war, although the Prince preferred sailing in the school schooner from Burghead.

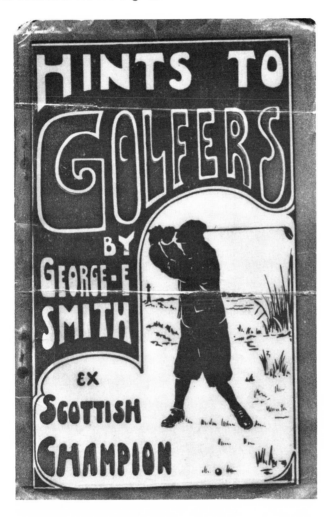

Willie Crockett returned from America and in 1934 became professional to the Royal Aberdeen golf club. He was succeeded at Balgownie in 1947 by John Campbell who, to his great delight, won the Scottish Professional Championship of 1952 over his own Lossiemouth links. In doing so he finished one shot ahead of the formidable seaside links player John Panton and put an end to a run of four successive victories by the Ryder Cup golfer.

Willie MacDonald remembers George Smith as a fine teacher, but a difficult man to work for as he was such a perfectionist. MacDonald spent seven years at Lossiemouth and then became assistant to James Adams at Hoylake before joining C.S. Denny as first assistant at Thorpe Hall. After war service in the Royal Marines he was appointed professional to Prestwick St Nicholas in 1946 and retired from there thirty-four years later. Willie was something of a perfectionist himself in his dress and his golf swing and had a very good record in post-war Scottish golf. In the Scottish Professional Championship he occupied the runner-up position on three occasions, he won the West of Scotland championship, and tied with George Will and Harry Weetman for the Northern Open championship, eventually losing the play-off to Will. He wore the plus-fours of the pre-war period with considerable dash and astonished a very large sergeant when he arrived at Chatham Barracks to join the Royal Marines attired in white plus-fours and black stockings.

W.S. MacDonald

George Smith was made an honorary member of the club on his retirement in 1950 and he was succeeded by James Neil Mackenzie who was professional at Baberton golf club near Edinburgh. He had served his apprenticeship at Lossiemouth before going to Langley Park golf club, Beckenham, Kent, in 1920 as first assistant to Frank Ball. In 1923 he was appointed professional to the Royal Antwerp golf club in Belgium where he remained for seventeen years and numbered Prince Leopold of the Belgians amongst his pupils and golfing companions. When war broke out he lost the entire contents of his shop and his flat and it took well over a month and repeated difficulties before he was able to reach Britain. James Mackenzie had lived in Lossiemouth from the age of twelve and he served with the county regiment — the Seaforth Highlanders — in both world wars. He was a very fine teacher, in spite of the arthritis which attacked his hands at an early age, and he took particular pains to organise classes and teach the very young — a policy which is still pursued enthusiastically by the resident professional at the Moray Golf Club. For many years he was teaching professional to Gordonstoun school, and he also was made an honorary member for his services to the golf club on his retirement in 1968.

Brian Anderson, an assistant with James Mackenzie, has had a distinguished professional career since leaving Lossiemouth. Appointed professional at Scotscraig golf club, Fife, he then accepted the post of

James Neil Mackenzie, Professional 1950-1968

professional to Helensburgh golf club where he remained for seventeen years and in 1986 he took up the challenging and prestigious post of professional to Dalmahoy Golf and Country club.

The professional from 1969-1974 was John R. Black from Yeovil in Somerset. John Black proved to be another of life's characters and he arrived in Lossiemouth via Royal Lytham & St Annes, St Annes Old Links, Wollaton Park, Nottingham, two Swedish clubs and a winter spent teaching at Lamco-Nimba golf club, Liberia, West Africa. Black was an enthusiastic and popular professional and a very good teacher with a keen sense of humour and a fund of unlikely stories. He still recalls the occasion when Captain Duncan Lang, R.N., was playing the eleventh hole and a helicopter landed on the course to take him to the air station for some emergency. However, Captain Lang decided he could not function properly without his jacket and walking shoes and the helicopter took him to the eighteenth green where he alighted and then was whisked off again to the control tower. Black listened to this story a few days later and then said to the Captain, "Well sir, I hope you realise that there's now no sand whatever left in Hell bunker."

Black went from Lossiemouth to Grangemouth and was appointed captain of the Scottish P.G.A. and is now professional to Tandragee golf club in Ulster.

One of the keenest assistant professionals at Moray was given his chance at a very early age by John Black. The eager and hard-working Frank Smith was taught every facet of his trade in the shop at Lossiemouth and then went on to Crieff as assistant to John Stark before being appointed full professional to Craigie Hill golf club in Perth in 1982.

The exciting amateur golfer Alistair Thomson, brother of the present captain, has been professional to the club for the past eleven years. A hard-working and convivial man and an excellent club professional, he now has less time for competitive golf as he is also teaching professional to the pupils of nearby Gordonstoun school. Even so, in the winter of 1987-88, he contrived to win the North of Scotland Golfers Alliance Championship with a succession of excellent rounds. Thomson follows faithfully in the tradition of Lossiemouth professionals as an excellent golf instructor and he continues the regular teaching of small children in large classes which was first begun by the late James Mackenzie.

CHAPTER X

Some Interesting Captains

THE portraits of past captains in the clubhouse attract a great deal of attention from visitors and members who frequently gaze at the photographs and wonder who and what they were. No account of the first hundred years of the Moray Golf Club would be complete without some reference to some of the personalities who played their part in its development.

The first captain and the main driving force in the formation of the golf club in 1889 was the Reverend Alexander Lawson. He was a very good golfer and captain of the club for two years. A graduate of the Universities of St Andrews and Heidelberg, he was a brilliant student and was capped M.A. with first class honours in Philosophy in 1874. He was the Tyndall-Bruce scholar at St Andrews in 1874 and Ramsay scholar in 1875 and took his B.D. in 1877. Lawson was collegiate minister in Elgin from 1882 and his passionate attachment to golf led not only to the foundation of the golf club but to the publication of one of the earliest instruction books which appeared as *Letters on Golf, by a Parish Minister* in 1889. (The author knows of one copy of this book still in existence. Another copy was sold by Phillips on 12th July 1988 for £8,400). The book was reviewed by the literary critic of *The Elgin Courant* in September 1889, and the writer observed:

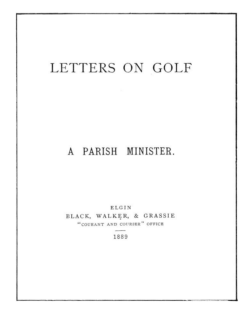

LETTERS ON GOLF

A PARISH MINISTER.

ELGIN
BLACK, WALKER, & GRASSIE
"COURANT AND COURIER" OFFICE
1889

Who does not like the breadth of view in the playful humour of a little speech by a Free Church minister who was also a first-class golfer? The reverend gentleman happened to win the medal of his Club, and had just been presented with the coveted honour. "My friends, I feel very much pleased, and indeed proud to be able to give you a good lesson not only from the pulpit on Sunday, but also on the links on this beautiful Saturday afternoon."

In 1893 Lawson moved on to the Parish of Deer in Aberdeenshire and in March 1897 he was appointed by the University Court to the new chair as Professor of English Literature at St Andrews University which he held until 1920. He was also Dean of the Arts Faculty at St Andrews and had many publications [to his name]. There appear to have been some initial difficulties over his appointment at St Andrews, and in its report of his inaugural address *The Northern Scot* of 9th October 1897 commented, "Mr Lawson was appointed to the English Literature chair by the majority of the University Court, the minority protesting against the legality of the Court and leaving the meeting prior to the appointment being made. The Senatus have, up to the present, refused to install Mr Lawson to the chair, and it is understood have brought the matter before the Privy Council." In 1904 Professor Lawson was made an honorary member of the Moray Golf Club and continued to play golf at Lossiemouth whenever possible.

The second captain appointed in 1890 was Dr George Mackay, who was in medical practice with his father Dr Norris Mackay of The Tower, Elgin, from 1883, but he died at the early age of thirty-six years. Various sea journeys had failed to restore his health.

John MacLeod, H.M.I.S., became captain in 1891, and continued the scholarly tradition. He was first prizeman in Natural Philosophy and Mathematics at the University of Glasgow under Professor Sir William Thomson — later Lord Kelvin — on whose recommendation MacLeod was appointed Professor of Mathematics at King's College, Windsor, Nova Scotia, in 1866, before he had even graduated at Glasgow. Three years later he returned to the mathematics department at Glasgow for some time and was subsequently appointed Instructor in Mathematics at the Royal Military Academy, Woolwich. When the Education Act in Scotland came into operation early in 1873, MacLeod was appointed to the staff of the Inspectorate and from 1877 he was Inspector of Schools for Caithness, Sutherland and Ross, and then for Moray and Nairn. He was captain of the golf club for a second term in 1901 and later received the Imperial Service Order from King Edward VII.

The captain in 1893 was an Elgin land-surveyor W. Monro MacBey, who drew up the plan for the original sixteen hole course which hangs in the clubhouse today. The first seven holes in this plan hugged the coast-line up to the Cooper ditch, but in the event the sixteen holes were constructed and played the reverse way. He was the first of four captains whose sons were also to become captains of the Moray Golf Club. His youngest son George, a Lieutenant in the 6th Seaforths who won the Military Cross, was killed near Arras in 1918 and his name is embossed on the fine cast bronze war memorial tablet with an oak surround on a wall in the clubhouse. This is the work of Charles Henshaw of Edinburgh and the following sentiment appears beneath the Roll of Honour. "They never fail who die in a great cause: They but augment the deep and sweeping thoughts which overpower all others and conduct the world at last to freedom."

William Christie, the enterprising hotelier, was the sixth captain in 1894. He was the tenant of the Stag Hotel in Commerce Street, Elgin, from 1876 until 1880 when he took over the Station Hotel. It was built by Provost Grant of Elgin as a hotel but was not successful and was transformed into a school called the Elgin Educational Institute. With the new proprietor's energy and initiative it reverted to a very successful hotel and enabled him to build the Stotfield Hotel at Lossiemouth in 1895. The construction

FOR GOLF PLAYERS

TO THE HONOURED MEMORY OF
THE MEMBERS OF THE MORAY
GOLF CLUB WHO GAVE THEIR LIVES
IN THE GREAT WAR 1914-1919

W. T. ANDERSON LT. SEAFORTHS & R.F.C.	E. C. J. HUMBERT LT. ROYAL BERKS REG.
P. T. G. BAIRD MAJ. CAMERONS	J. T. JENKINS LT. SEAFORTHS
H. W. F. BARTON LT. ROYAL SCOTS FUS.	C. E. JOHNSTON, D.S.O. MAJ. SEAFORTHS
E. L. S. BENNETT MAJ. 66TH PUNJABIS	E. J. F. JOHNSTON CAPT. ROYAL SCOTS
G. C. COLLIER LT. SCOT RIFS.	I. R. KEITH LT. SH PRIN PATRICIAS C.L.I.
L. R. CUMMING LT. THE BLACK WATCH	G. MESSERVY, M.C. MAJ. R.F.A.
F. G. FLEMING, M.C. CAPT. GORDONS	E. D. MESSERVY CAPT. LOND. REG. & R.F.C.
W. J. G. FLEMING CAPT. GORDONS	G. M. MACBEY, M.C. LT. SEAFORTHS
W. F. FORSYTH CAPT. 28TH CANADIANS	C. NEILSON C.S.M. GORDONS
I. B. GALLOWAY MAJ. SEAFORTHS	J. L. SIM PTE. SEAFORTHS
R. S. GORDON MAJ. 57TH WILDE'S RIF. F.F.	D. STEWART LT. SEAFORTHS
G. D. GORDON LT. NORTHANTS REG.	FLEETWOOD THORNE CAPT. GRENADIER GDS.
L. GORDON DUFF CAPT. GORDONS	A. T. WELSH LT. ROYAL WELCH FUS.
B. H. GORDON LENNOX MAJ. GRENADIER GDS.	G. C. WEST SGT. LANARK YEO.
J. N. GOURLAY LT. SEAFORTHS	R. S. WILSON CAPT. SEAFORTHS

of the Stotfield was a long drawn-out business as a severe frost prevented the masons doing a hand's turn for twelve weeks. The river Lossie at Elgin was frozen over from Deanshaugh to Sheriffmill and during those twelve weeks anyone who cared to could take a short cut over the Lossie in perfect safety.

Christie ran the two hotels in harness until 1900 when he sold the Elgin one and devoted his great energies to the flourishing Stotfield Hotel. He played a considerable part in the development of Lossiemouth as a prosperous holiday resort, and when he retired in 1924 and sold the Stotfield to John McCulloch, his son-in-law, the original sixteen bedrooms had increased to almost seventy. A very good golfer when he had the time — he won the Pitgaveny medal in 1890 and his is the first name on the Hon. John Gordon cup in 1897 — he was also a member of the Lossiemouth Town Council for twenty-two years and Provost for seven years. Like so many early members and captains he was a very prominent Freemason. His first house in Lossiemouth was Laverockbank, now a hotel, and he used it in the summer to accommodate the overflow from the Stotfield. He gave a great deal of his time to the well-being of the

John MacLeod H.M.I.S.

W. Monro MacBey

William Christie Snr.

John B. Mair M.V.O., O.B.E.

Moray Golf Club, and countless members and a host of visitors to Lossiemouth looked on him as a personal friend. His second daughter Cissie married David West the Lossiemouth artist.

A prominent Elgin lawyer in James McIsaac became captain in 1895. He joined the Elgin legal firm of Forsyth and Stewart in 1882, and some years after David Forsyth's death in 1885 the firm became known as Stewart and McIsaac, and is carried on under this title at the present day. James McIsaac was a founder member of the golf club and a scratch golfer, and it comes as no great surprise to discover that the man who formed the first Moray Golf Club on 2nd April 1875 was the then senior partner, David Forsyth. McIsaac was noted for his forensic abilities and rapidly acquired a reputation as a successful pleader in the courts, and it was he who attempted to restrain John Foster when the question of Ramsay MacDonald's expulsion first arose in August 1915.

Dr John Taylor of Elgin was captain of the club at the end of the nineteenth century. He was educated at Elgin Academy and Aberdeen University and returned to Elgin in 1892 where he soon built up a large practice. He was one of the old school of general practitioner surgeons and from 1903 he was senior surgeon at Dr Gray's Hospital in Elgin for thirty-five years.

In 1902 John Baigrie Mair was elected to the captaincy. A big man of great energy and not a little power, he was Chief Constable of the county of Moray from 1892 until his death in 1927 at the age of seventy. He was very active in the community and further afield and one his main interests in which he held high office was Freemasonry. He was also well-known for the numerous charities he started and carried on for many years. He was responsible for the elaborate police arrangements which were necessary when King Edward VII visited the Sassoons at Tulchan Lodge on Speyside, but although Mrs Sassoon was a member of the Moray Golf Club and frequently brought her guests to play golf, there is no evidence that the King ever came to Lossiemouth. Not surprisingly, in September 1909 John Mair was decorated by King Edward with the Royal Victorian Order, and on other occasions he was the recipient of valuable gifts from members of the Royal family. He was also responsible for the security arrangements when King George V and his family stayed with the Duke of Richmond and Gordon at Gordon Castle at Fochabers, and he was made an O.B.E. for his work during the first war. John Mair served on the Council of the golf club for many years and over a long period was the organiser of the New Year's day competition which was inaugurated in 1896. In this unique competition almost everyone brought a prize and everyone got a prize. Pheasants by the brace, gloves, scarves, woollen sweaters, travelling rugs, bottles of wine and whisky, golf clubs, golf balls, boxes of cigarettes, and many other handsome prizes were borne home in triumph by the successful competitors. The competition continues in a much modified form to the present day.

John Mair was of humble origin and was very proud of the fact that he was one of four ploughmen on the farm of Broadland, Cairnie, Aberdeenshire, all of whom rose to the rank of Chief Constable.

It is significant that the founder members used the home of the Trinity Lodge of Freemasons in the Assembly Rooms in Elgin for the initial meeting to form the golf club on 13th March 1889. The great majority of the eighty-two founding members were almost certainly Freemasons, an assumption made more certain by the high proportion of professional

John Sim

John F. Cumming

Sheriff James G. Webster

Colonel C.J. Johnston

106

men amongst them, and from information gleaned from local newspapers of the time. Trinity Lodge in Elgin has always been the traditional home of successful professional men and equally successful businessmen. In a recently published book, David Stirk acknowledges the debt owed to Freemasons in keeping the game alive in the mid-nineteenth century and has this to say about them.

> Given that they were a secret society and must remain so, praise is due to them for keeping the game alive and bringing the benefits of properly organised Clubs, keen and fair competitions and formal rules of play to a game which had hitherto been played pretty haphazardly. For though the Masons started playing golf as an adjunct to having bets and as a means of working up an appetite, it was not long before they were bitten by the allure of the game itself and became keen players.

Freemasons in Morayshire were more open in their activities and membership and bore little resemblance to the secret Masonic lodges of the cities. The most un-Masonic like action of the Moray Golf Club was the early admission of women members, notwithstanding the restrictions imposed on them. Whilst there was no problem in keeping ladies out of the Masonic Lodge, there was a distinct problem in preventing them taking up a healthy open-air pursuit such as golf. Moreover, the Council of the golf club provided accommodation for them in the clubhouse at an early stage, and they still enjoy the privilege of one of the best rooms in the club with a glorious view over the first and eighteenth fairways and a sweeping vista of the landscape from north to south. With the post-war decline in the membership of the ladies section, successive Councils have cast their eyes on their quarters and it has now been decreed that the Ladies lounge is to be known as the Upstairs lounge. This is all very well as far as it goes, but, until the dining-room and the bar are moved to the first floor, it is unlikely that anyone but the ladies will use the Upstairs lounge.

The first Lossiemouth man to become captain in the sixteenth year of the club's existence in 1904 was John Sim the draper. With his tidy beard, high collar, and tweed suit with cap to match he is immediately recognisable in a number of photographs in the possession of the club.

John Fleetwood Cumming was captain in 1905-07 and for a second time in 1919-22. He succeeded his father as proprietor of Cardhu distillery at Knockando and carried on the farm of Cardow as well as tenanting Kinermony where he built up a very successful herd of Aberdeen Angus cattle. The herd was sold before his death in 1933 but when Sainsbury's became the tenants of Kinermony after the second war another fine Angus herd was established there which also enjoyed considerable success. John Cumming was yet another energetic captain who found time for many and numerous activities. Practically from the passing of the Local Government Act in 1888 he was associated with the Moray County Council and was eventually convener of Morayshire for nine years, succeeding another member of the golf club, G.R. Mackessack of Ardgye. His home was The Dowans at Aberlour, and he owned a large summer residence, Eastcliff in Lossiemouth, which stands above the present second and eighteenth tees of the Old course.

Cumming was a crack shot with a sporting gun and a very fine golfer as well as an able administrator, and his terms of office coincided with periods of very rapid expansion at the Moray Golf Club. His first captaincy from 1905-7 was notable for the considerable extension of the first nine holes of the Old course and the construction of the new nine-hole Relief course which was opened for play in July 1906. His second term in 1919-22

Sir Alexander Grant, Baronet.
From the portrait in The Tolbooth, Forres

saw another (post-war) golf resurgence and many important changes at the golf club.

In 1920, Alexander Grant of Edinburgh offered a loan of three thousand pounds, free of interest for ten years, to build a second eighteen hole course. The Council had doubts about the necessity of a second eighteen holes, and when Cumming visited Grant in London he informed him of this. Grant's reply was to offer a gift to the club of two hundred and fifty pounds for another purpose, namely to alter the first hole of the Old course as recommended by Grant's great friend, the professional Ted Ray. (Ted Ray and Harry Vardon were the only British golfers to win both the Open Championship and the U.S. Open Championship until joined by Tony Jacklin in 1970). This gift was gratefully accepted and was followed by a suggestion that Grant's company, McVitie & Price, would sponsor a professional tournament at Lossiemouth in June 1920 with prize money of five hundred pounds. Alexander Grant and Ted Ray were close friends and Ray was often a guest of Grant's at the Marine Hotel in Lossiemouth where the latter kept a suite of rooms for much of the year.

John Cumming was fortunate to have a practical Council which contained another distiller, a farmer, a banker, two businessmen and no fewer than six lawyers including the secretary. Alexander Grant's idea for a tournament which would put Lossiemouth on the golfing map was quickly taken up, and the tournaments of 1920 and 1922 enabled the captain to have meetings on the course with James Braid, Ted Ray, Aubrey Boomer of St Cloud and George Duncan. The famous professionals discussed each hole and suggested numerous improvements. Again in 1920 Alexander Grant offered to advance money on easy terms for the reconstruction of the clubhouse and the Council accepted this with alacrity. He also intimated that the McVitie & Price tournament had been so successful that he would put up the prize money in 1922 provided it was again played at Lossiemouth. Alexander Grant was made an honorary member of the Moray Golf Club on 5th April 1920, a well-merited distinction.

Cumming's three sons and a daughter were all members of the golf club. Captain Lewis Cumming of the Black Watch was killed in the war and Captain John Kynoch Cumming became the second Moray golfer after George Thomson to win the Northern Amateur Championship at Lossiemouth in 1920, the first tournament held after the war years. Kynoch Cumming had been severely wounded during the war and taken prisoner, and he never completely recovered and died at the early age of thirty-one years. The second son Ronald Cumming played rugby for Scotland and became chairman of the Distillers Company Limited and received a knighthood. Cumming's daughter, Mrs Miller-Stirling, and her husband spent their holidays for many years at Eastcliff and she returned to the Moray Golf Club a year or two ago when well over eighty years of age to play over the course and put in three cards for a handicap.

The next captain in 1907 was James G. Webster, Sheriff-Substitute of Inverness, Elgin and Nairn. He had been Sheriff-Substitute at Lochmaddy on North Uist in the Outer Hebrides from 1881-99 and was the prime mover in the formation of a golf course there. The course at Lochmaddy was said to be one of the finest in Scotland but it is no longer in existence. The Sheriff was known as a kind man with more than a local reputation as a judge and he was a most enthusiastic and generous member of the golf club.

He was followed in 1909 by Colonel Charles J. Johnston, V.D., T.D., who was born in 1845 in his grandfather's home Newmill House, Elgin, and became a partner in the family firm of James Johnston & Co., woollen manufacturers, Newmill. He later lived in Lesmurdie House and then in The Craig at Lossiemouth. Charles Johnston was a keen part-time soldier and joined the Elgin and Lhanbryde Volunteers as a private in 1861 and rose to command the battalion in 1894. By that time it had become the 3rd volunteer battalion of the Seaforth Highlanders under its previous Colonel, Sir Felix Mackenzie of Forres, and when Colonel Johnston relinquished his command nine years later he was appointed honorary Colonel of his battalion, now the 6th Seaforths. As a young Lieutenant he was in charge of the guard of honour on the Highland station at Elgin on September 6th 1872 when Queen Victoria, on her way from Balmoral to Dunrobin Castle, halted her train for a few minutes to receive a loyal address and glimpse the cathedral city from her window in the Royal saloon.

[Colonel] Johnston was a founder member of the golf club, a member of the Elgin Town Council and a very prominent Freemason in the county of Moray. He was a pioneer of the Boy Scout movement in Moray and when he died in 1940 at his home in Lossiemouth in his ninety-fifth year he was the oldest scout in Great Britain. In 1904 no fewer than seven male Johnstons of Lesmurdie were listed as members of the golf club.

Major Sir Alistair Gordon Cumming Bt., M.C., on whose land the golf course lay west of the Cooper ditch, was captain in 1933. He was the eldest son of Sir William Gordon Cumming of Gordonstoun and Altyre who had married an American lady, Miss Florence Josephine Garner of New York, on the day after the verdict in the Baccarat case. This celebrated case took place in London in 1891 and was the result of an action for slander raised by Sir William against a number of defendants. At the time of the events which led to the action, Sir William Gordon Cumming was a forty-two year old bachelor and a Lieut. Colonel in the Scots Guards with a distinguished record in the Zulu War and in campaigns in Egypt and Sudan. He owned estates of more than thirty thousand acres in Scotland and newspaper reports of the time put his income at

Sir Alistair Gordon Cumming

more than £60,000 per annum. He was also a friend of the Prince of Wales of some twenty years standing, and at the Prince's behest he found himself a member of a house party at Tranby Croft near Doncaster, the home of a Mr and Mrs Wilson.

The Prince of Wales had brought his Baccarat counters with him and Baccarat was played on two successive nights with the Prince as the banker. Sir William was no stranger to the game which has been described as the easiest way to lose, or win, money, and all the members of the party appear to have taken part. One of the young men present thought he observed Sir William cheating on the first night and other members of the party, who had been appraised of this and warned to look out, also thought he cheated on the second night. Two senior members of the house party, one a Lord and the other a General, were told of this and approached the Prince of Wales. The outcome was that Sir William was accused of cheating, which he vehemently denied, but he then signed a document stating that he would never play cards again and it was solemnly declared that the document would never become public. Ten other signatures were appended, headed by that of the Prince of Wales.

Within a short time it was the talk of London and Sir William began his famous action for slander on 1st June 1891 in the Lord Chief Justice's Court. Sir Charles Russell Q.C., M.P., and Herbert Asquith Q.C., M.P., represented the defendants and the Solicitor-General Sir Edward Clarke Q.C., led for the plaintiff. After a week of intense public interest in the case, in which the Prince sat in a special chair beside the Lord Chief Justice and lunched with him at the appointed hour, the jury found in favour of the defendants. The verdict proved unpopular at the time and particularly so in the north of Scotland where it was never believed that Sir William was guilty of cheating. Florence Garner arranged her wedding to Sir William on the day after the verdict and insisted on going through with the ceremony without bridesmaids or any member of her family present. Sir William was ostracised by society, lost his rank in the Guards and retired to his Scottish estates. The citizens of Forres, who did not care much for the English at the best of times, spent a good deal of the night decorating their railway station and laid on a civic reception for Sir William and his American bride, and when they arrived they pulled their landau through the streets. Queen Victoria cannot have been amused.

Sir William Gordon Cumming on the first tee — 1893

111

Two of the principals in this case became closely associated with the new Moray Golf Club. In 1894 Herbert Asquith married Margot Tennant of Innes House and both became prominent members of the golf club. Sir William Gordon Cumming also became a prominent member, and as a keen golfer and proprietor of part of the course, he was given precedence at the first tee for his generosity to the club.

The captain for three years from 1935 was a man who had no liking for a quiet life. Lt. Colonel J.E. (Edward) Tennant of Innes House was a second lieutenant in the Scots Guards at the outbreak of the Great War and speedily had himself transferred to the new Royal Flying Corps in 1914. He served in France until 1916, and then as commanding officer of the R.F.C. (later the R.A.F.) in Mesopotamia where he was shot down and captured, and then rescued five days later by an armoured car sent to find him. Mentioned in despatches five times, awarded the D.S.O. and M.C. and created a Chevalier de la Légion d'Honneur, he finished the war as Director of Aeronautics in India and wrote a book entitled *In the Clouds above Baghdad.* After the war his hunting expeditions took him to the White Nile, the Sinai peninsula and India, and he was a member of the Oxford University Arctic Expedition to North East Land in 1924. For recreation he indulged in yachting, shooting and golf, and as captain and green convener at the Moray

Lt Colonel J.E. Tennant

Golf Club he and the professional George Smith were responsible for many important alterations to the golf course. Col. Tennant's father, Francis Tennant, was a good friend to the golf club and in June 1928 made an unpublicised gift of the first motor tractor, a Gun-Joey, to replace the horse-drawn mower then in use.

Many well-known personalities and golfers were guests of the Tennants at Innes House during the golf season and played regularly over the links at Lossiemouth. The Duchess of Rutland and Lady (Margot) Asquith, sisters of Francis Tennant, were frequent visitors. Lady Asquith made an impression on one of the young assistant professionals employed by George Smith who still recalls her vivacity and her colourful style of dressing, although he was rather shocked to see her smoking a cigarette when playing off the first tee. Major C.K. Hutchison, runner-up in the British Amateur Championship of 1909, was a frequent visitor as was Joyce Wethered. Five times English Ladies' and four times British Ladies' Amateur Champion, Joyce Wethered also made a successful tour of the

United States and played in a remarkable match in Atlanta, Georgia. The match took place at East Lake, the home course of Bobby Jones, where Charlie Yates and Miss Wethered played Jones and Miss Dorothy Kirby of Atlanta. According to Keeler, no concessions were made to the ladies and Jones holed a five yard putt on the last green to halve the match. Jones had beaten Miss Wethered by two and one and she in turn had beaten Yates by one hole. Keeler reports Yates's reaction. "I still don't believe it," said Charlie. "No girl can hit a ball that far. [That's the] first time I ever played fourteen holes as a lady's partner before I figured once in the match; or four holes for that matter. Reckon I should have been pretty embarrassed but I was sort of hypnotized watching her play." Yates was no slouch on the golf course as his record as top amateur in the Masters at Augusta in 1934-39-40 confirms, and he was British Amateur Champion in 1938.

In the second world war Edward Tennant was a Group Captain in the R.A.F. and personal secretary to Sir Charles Portal, Chief of the Air Staff, and he was killed in a flying accident in 1941 at fifty-one years of age.

Major George Boyd Anderson, M.C., M.B.E., was a great friend and benefactor of the golf club who was captain in 1948. He lived for very many years in Skerrybrae, now an hotel, an imposing dwelling bordering the eighteenth fairway. Although he was a man of independent means he worked for many years as a rubber merchant in Singapore, and he was particularly noted for his great generosity. To the town of Elgin he gave the Rose nursery school and playground in memory of his parents, and later the magnificent gift of the beautiful estate of Millbuies. He established a playing field in Lossiemouth and donated the pavilion, and gave the British Legion their premises. At the golf club he refurbished the lounge and spent a large sum of money on improving the then nine-hole relief course, and the golf course architect C.K. Cotton was a frequent guest at Skerrybrae.

When the new road through the golf course to Hopeman was mooted, Boyd Anderson was strongly against it from the start. He gave a handsome donation for counsel to represent the club at the subsequent enquiry, and, when the road went through, he left Lossiemouth in 1957 for Edinburgh and gave his beautiful home, Skerrybrae, to the Order of St John of Jerusalem to be used as a convalescent home. Among his many bequests he paid the total cost of the original White Lady Shieling on Cairngorm and made substantial contributions for improvements to it when it belonged to the National Trust. He also paid for the Lagganlia Outdoor Education Centre at Kincraig which he gifted to Edinburgh Corporation, and he was the donor of the Boyd Anderson trophy for ski-ing among secondary schools in Moray, Nairn and Banff. Boyd Anderson's somewhat impish sense of humour was in evidence even at his funeral service in St Margaret's church at Lossiemouth where he had left the following instructions:

> It is my wish that everyone attending my funeral service be invited to drink to my "departed spirit" at the Moray Golf Club.

The very great majority of those who were present accepted the invitation in the spirit in which it was extended, and the general opinion was that Boyd, as he was affectionately known, had set a precedent which might well be emulated by others.

Major George Boyd Anderson

Three prominent members of the Moray Golf Club came together in a very unusual court case in Elgin in 1938. They were Major Boyd Anderson, Sheriff A.F. Hamilton Grierson (who was to be captain in 1946) and David West, although the latter had been dead for eighteen months.

In 1936 Boyd Anderson had been making further alterations to Skerrybrae, his elaborate home alongside the eighteenth fairway, with its specially designed cocktail bar and indoor swimming pond, which were unusual features for the area. The house was known locally as "lipstick villa" as the window frames were painted with red paint instead of the more conventional white. His friend David West the artist was frequently consulted on the artistic decoration of the house during the alterations and it was arranged between them that West would paint pictures for three of the windows — but on the inside of window blinds. The

Sheriff A.F. Hamilton Grierson

scenes selected for the pictures were Covesea Lighthouse, a scene from the Tunnel Brae, Aberlour, and a moorland scene including Ben Rinnes in Banffshire. The paintings took about five weeks of work and Boyd Anderson admitted that he was delighted with them. He said that from the outside of the house the effect was rather extraordinary and that when the lights were put on inside the house, a crowd of people gathered outside to look at the paintings, illuminated from the inside.

The problem was that a price did not appear to have been fixed beforehand and the trustees of the late David West sued Boyd Anderson for £150, and he in turn offered £50. The evidence lasted all day in Elgin Sheriff court and for the trustees two prominent Scottish artists expressed the opinion that the paintings, which were used as decorative window blinds, were of a high standard and "typical David West" pictures. Two well-known art dealers gave evidence that the work was inferior to West's usual work. In his judgment Sheriff Hamilton Grierson felt that the artist thought that the paintings were worthy of him and had expressed his opinion of them by signing them, and that the defender and his friends appeared to have considered the paintings of considerable value. He accordingly assessed their value at £120, but since their use as window blinds would shorten their permanence as paintings, he awarded the trustees the sum of £96. Many years later, when Skerrybrae had reverted to private ownership, the blinds were taken down and framed as pictures and sold at public auction.

David West

David West was an interesting character. He was born in 1868, the youngest of twelve children, and was educated at Lossiemouth, Elgin Academy and Aberdeen Grammar School. He received no formal training in art but later in his life he went to Holland to study the work of the Dutch Masters. After leaving school he went to sea, and then became involved in the Klondike Gold Rush, but failed to make his fortune there. He began work as a professional artist before he set off for the Yukon, and by 1894 his pictures had been accepted and hung at the Royal Academy for five successive years and he was a regular exhibitor at the Royal Scottish Academy. His first studio was at 11, Pitgaveny Street in Lossiemouth but on the 26th September 1897 it was destroyed by fire and dozens of his paintings, including many oils, were lost. In 1903 he was chosen by the Society of Scottish Artists as one of their representatives at the Munich Exhibition, and in 1927 he was invited to the Argentine where he was the first British artist to hold a successful exhibition of his water-colours in the capital, Buenos Aires. Although predominantly a local — and largely seascape — artist, one of his most famous paintings is a Dutch landscape entitled "On the Scheldt" which was hung at Edinburgh in 1932.

David West married a local girl, Cissie Christie, the daughter of William Christie of the Stotfield Hotel, and his interests were many and varied. He was a scratch golfer, enjoyed shooting and fishing and was an active member of the community and served on many local committees including the Council of the golf club and Lossiemouth Town Council. He was particularly interested in education and was a member of the old School Board, and at a later date, of the long defunct Education Authority. The house which was his second studio still stands below the clubhouse on the north side and bears the name "Chilkoot", named after the Chilkoot Pass Mountain in British Columbia where the Yukon river has its source. David West and his companions had slept on the summit of the great Chilkoot pass on 13th and 14th May 1898 on their way to the Klondike. *The Banffshire Herald* of 18th June 1898 published the thirty year-old West's account from Alaska under the heading "On the way to the Klondyke".

> Camped at Lake Inderman, Alaska, May 23rd 1898. We got through the great Chilkoot pass safely, and saw the great snowslide where so many were killed. The heat today was great and the snow and ice are going fast, and in a few days we will be in our canoes and on the way to the 'Golden Yukon'. I hope I'll pull through whether I have gold or not. I can hardly get peace to write for a young Yank laying off yarns about his father and uncle in the American [Civil] War. I am in grand health and I feel fit. The scenery is grand and I'll have a good stock of sketches, and with my Kodak camera I'll have something worth.

West's adventurous spirit was seen again in the First Great War when, nearing fifty years of age, he managed to get close to the front lines driving a Banffshire ambulance and sent back racy accounts of his adventures which were published in *The Banffshire Advertiser*.

His fertile imagination conceived the construction of a jetty for pleasure boats at the Hythe, — that beautiful natural harbour below the golf clubhouse — and he drew up the plans in 1895 but the jetty was never built. In the same year that he patented his tee box, he also patented a buoy for communication between vessels or a stranded ship and the shore. David West was invited, along with artists such as Nicholson, Orpen and Munnings, to contribute a miniature painting for the Queen's Dolls' House, designed by the architect Sir Edwin Lutyens, and given in 1923 to H.M. Queen Mary as a symbol of national goodwill. In the autumn of 1936 he attended a Royal Academy Exhibition in Glasgow, but on 7th October he was taken ill and died before he could make the journey home.

116

Dr Joseph Chasser Jessop (1892-1972) became captain in 1950. Appointed headmaster in 1933 of Lossiemouth Junior Secondary School, for long the school with the biggest roll in Moray and Nairn, he was a native of Montrose and a graduate of St Andrews University where he was captain of the golf team. His career was interrupted by the Great War in which

Dr J.C. Jessop

he was an officer in the Black Watch and was wounded while serving with the 51st Highland Division. Jessop first made his mark in amateur golfing circles at the age of sixteen by winning the county championship of Angus in which he was again successful on two subsequent occasions. He reached the last eight of the British Amateur in 1913 and was good enough to play in the Open Championship. In 1923 he reached the last eight of the Scottish Amateur Championship at Troon and his great friend Arthur Havers, professional at Coombe Hill, won the Open Championship in the same year and also at Troon. Arthur Gladstone Havers — a nephew of W.H. Havers of Hopeman in Moray — was a frequent visitor to "Seaholme", the Jessop home in Lossiemouth. He and Dr Jessop often talked of the events of that year which was also marked by the birth of Jessop's twin daughters. One of his daughters, Frances (Mrs W.M. Souter), survives him and lives in Inverness. She is a member of the executive committee of the S.L.G.A. and in that capacity will be present at Lossiemouth in 1989 for the Scottish Ladies' Amateur Championship, the fourth time it will have been played over the Moray links.

Dr Jessop won the Moray Open amateur tournament on four occasions, the first in 1934 at the age of forty-two and the last in 1949 at the age of fifty-seven, and defeated some distinguished golfers in the process. His outstanding golfing ability and scholarship led to an invitation from the publishers of the Teach Yourself series of books to write *Teach Yourself Golf* in 1950, and this book is still in print and currently in its sixth edition. The then golf correspondent of *The Glasgow Herald* thought very highly of his book and it received a favourable review from S.L. McKinlay writing in *The Bulletin*. Peter Dobereiner of the *Observer* gave it an honourable mention in one of his weekly articles, surely an accolade from the heir to Bernard Darwin and Henry Longhurst as a writer on golfing matters.

TEACH YOURSELF BOOKS

J. C. Jessop

GOLF

It remains an excellent book of instruction for the beginner and for golfers who are in difficulties with some part of their game, although since Jessop's death in 1972 some of his pithier stories have been edited out in favour of quotations (duller, in the author's view) from leading modern professionals. In the original text Jessop related the story of Sandy Herd playing at Carnoustie with Andrew Kirkaldy as his caddie. As Herd was approaching his ball about to play his second shot, Kirkaldy handed him his brassie. "Give me my cleek, Andra," said Sandy, "I haven't got a very good stance." "Play your brassie," brusquely retorted Kirkaldy. "You play this game wi' yer heid, no' yer feet." Jessop also commented that some amateurs can drive as far as the leading professionals, although their iron play was inferior, and added Andrew Kirkaldy's caustic remark, "Any d - - - - d fool can drive." He also quoted J.H. Taylor's advice on the approach shot that "There are no hazards in the air", a maxim which has been enthusiastically adopted by today's leading golfers who fly their approach shots to the green with wedges or sand-irons.

Dr Jessop had a distinguished University career being first prizeman in Education and graduating M.A. with first class honours. He was well known in scholarly circles for his Ph.D. thesis *A History of Education in Angus* which was later published as a monograph, and he was elected a Fellow of the Royal Historical Society for his *Researches into Scottish History.* Curiously enough his ambition as a young man was to become a professional golfer, an uncertain occupation in those days, but he was persuaded by his father to go to St Andrews University and finish his education in the traditional Scottish manner. This early unfulfilled ambition and his keen life-long interest in all aspects of golf led to many long and happy friendships with some of the leading professionals who frequently stayed with him at Lossiemouth. Harry Vardon was his boyhood hero and Jessop had played an exhibition match with him in 1919 at Montrose. Arthur Havers and Abe Mitchell were his old golfing companions and Jessop numbered Dai Rees, Bill Shankland, Max Faulkner, Charlie Ward and Fred Daly among his friends. The parents of the late Eric Brown spent their holidays in Montrose and the young Brown was a great follower of Dr Jessop in his Montrose days, and many years later stayed with the Jessops while playing in the Northern Open at Lossiemouth. Apart from his book on golf, Dr Jessop was the author of numerous newspaper articles on golf and golfers, a task for which he was well qualified as he played golf to scratch or better for forty-one years.

William Christie Jnr., a retired banker, was the second generation of Christie's to become captain in 1952. His father owned Laverockbank as well as the Stotfield Hotel, and had built the house known as Ley Lodge as a retirement home halfway between the two buildings. His son also retired to Ley Lodge and became convener of the Moray and Nairn Joint County Council as well as captain of the golf club. In his youth at Lossiemouth he had played off a handicap of plus two and he and George Thomson had vied for the top honours at the Moray Golf Club. The first two names on the unusual and handsome cup presented by the Hon. John Gordon M.P. in 1897 are William Christie Snr. and William Christie Jnr..

The captain from 1955 to 1957 was Robert G. (Roy) Tulloch, for many years principal teacher of Physics at Elgin Academy and Provost of Lossiemouth for three years from 1961. In 1955, due to an administrative blunder, the Moray Golf Club failed to elect a captain and Roy Tulloch as vice-captain chaired the Council meetings for twelve months. It proved impossible to correct this under the constitution of the club as it then stood, and the permanent officials and officers of the golf club had difficulty in disguising their embarrassment. Roy Tulloch was responsible for the policy of building large teeing grounds for easier maintenance and dispensing with the necessity for winter tees. He was also numbered as one of the pioneers of the New course and he played an enthusiastic part in the building of a second eighteen hole course.

Robert G. (Roy) Tulloch

The most senior living captain from 1957-1959 is John Stewart of Lossiemouth who succeeded George Cursiter. Cursiter, an Elgin dentist, was the third captain to die in office, the others being Dr George Smith Sowden of Elgin in 1929 and Captain P. Kynoch Shand in 1939.

Major Innes Matheson, T.D., J.P., was captain in 1961-63 and for a second term in 1967-69. Educated at Inverness and Edinburgh Academy, he served with the Highland Division and was twice wounded in the last war after which he settled in business in Lossiemouth. Apart from the golf club, Innes Matheson was chairman of the Lossiemouth branch of the Royal British Legion for many years, a member of the Moray and Nairn Joint County Council and the last Provost of Lossiemouth prior to the re-organisation of local government. A determined character both on and off the golf course, he was never afraid to speak his mind and he was an outspoken critic of the necessity for a second eighteen hole course. Innes Matheson was a stern competitor on the golf course even before he acquired a somewhat odd putter with a red-painted broad head, closely resembling the old Schenectady putter. With this unlikely club he acquired a fearsome reputation for his infallibility on the putting green, and, as the records testify, he proceeded to win the club championship and a host of matchplay events over the years. He still has a great enthusiasm for the game and he and his senior friends can be seen on the golf course all the year round.

Another Provost of Lossiemouth, the urbane Sandy Edwards, was captain in 1963-65. He is a nephew of Sergeant Alexander Edwards who won the Victoria Cross in the First World War and is commemorated on the sundial on the slope above the eighteenth green of the Old course. When his uncle's V.C. came into his possession he had no hesitation in presenting it to the Seaforth Highlanders regimental museum. Apart from his term of office as captain, Sandy Edwards has been a hard-working member of the old Lossiemouth Town Council and the Council of the golf club over many years, and when he had time from his many business and other commitments to apply himself on the golf course, he won, among other things the coveted Pitgaveny gold medal. He still plays regularly on Saturdays in a four-ball match which dines at the ninth hole on smoked salmon washed down with the wine of the golf club.

Ernest Kintrea Christie of The Craig, Lossiemouth, grandson of William Christie of the Stotfield Hotel, was captain in 1975-76 and honorary treasurer from 1978 until his death in 1986. Named after Ernest Kintrea, his father's friend and scratch golfer at the Moray Golf Club, "Kin" Christie was himself a very fine golfer in his younger day. A chartered accountant who spent much of his life in the Far East, he applied his wealth of financial and administrative expertise and shrewd judgment to the running of the golf club and in 1985 he was made an honorary member for his services to the club.

E.K. (Kin) Christie

PAST CAPTAINS
Back Row: **Dr J.A. McConachie, Dr G.D. Gormley, I.Macdonald, J. Campbell, J. Stephen, R.A. Conti, J. Harris**
Front Row: **W.F. Thomson, J. Stewart, P.N. O'Brien, I.M. Matheson, S.J. Edwards**

In recent years the names of some captains have been associated with specific changes and events in the history of the golf club. James Campbell and Innes Macdonald are prominently associated with the construction of the New course and Dr George Gormley is a well-known and hard-working official of the Scottish Golf Union. James Stephen's name will always be linked with the important structural changes he made to the interior of the clubhouse during his captaincy, Robert Conti bought a large amount of modern machinery for the courses while asserting that he was preserving the status quo, and John Harris was responsible for obtaining substantial sponsorship for the club's Open tournaments and putting them on a business-like footing. Great efforts have been made to improve the New course in the last few years and bring it up to the standard of the Old, and the credit for this is largely due to Patrick O'Brien.

The captain in Centenary year is schoolmaster W. Farquhar Thomson. This is his third term as captain of the golf club, having first been elected to the post in 1965 at the tender age — for a captain — of twenty-nine years. A man of great energy and organising ability, he is also secretary of the North of Scotland Alliance, chairman of the Moray and Nairn Golf League and vice-chairman of the Northern Scottish Open Championship committee. He can take most of the credit for the New course, which would not have been built without his vision and drive, and it is fitting that he should once again be captain as the Moray Golf Club enters its second hundred years. Farquhar Thomson was a scratch golfer for a number of years and contested many open tournament finals at Moray, Peterhead, Strathlene (Buckie), Forres and Banff. He has won his share of tournaments and trophies, but it is as an administrator that he excels and his infectious enthusiasm for the club of which he is such an outstanding member shines through all his actions.

121

No. 1 .	Rock,	389 yds.
„ 2 .	Covesea,	385 „
„ 3 .	Pitgaveny,	284 „
„ 4 .	Skerry Cliff,	480 „
„ 5 .	Cup,	293 „
„ 6 .	Table,	374 „
„ 7 .	Drainie,	242 „
„ 8 .	Gordonstoun,	350 „
„ 9 .	Ditch,	390 „
„ 10 .	St. Gerardine,	265 „
„ 11 .	Lighthouse,	212 „
„ 12 .	Target,	258 „
„ 13 .	V,	446 „
„ 14 .	Sea,	267 „
„ 15 .	Short,	162 „
„ 16 .	Road,	362 „
„ 17 .	Long,	512 „
„ 18 .	Mt. Lebanon,	387 „

Plan of the course given to Stotfield Hotel guests — 1895

122

CHAPTER XI

Development of the Courses

WHEN the original eighteen holes of the Old course were laid out, the first and second holes were played along the line of the gardens to the second green near the rock in the garden of The Craig, and the second hole was named "The Rock". The teeing ground for the first hole was situated on the high ground where the present clubhouse stands. The first hole was eventually lengthened to the Rock green, the second and third holes were played out towards Covesea lighthouse, and the fourth hole came back to the Skerrycliff green below Skerrycliff [cottage]. The fifth hole, "The Cup", was played to the same green as the second hole today. In 1895 the first hole was again altered and was played from a tee on the first fairway to the Rock green. The eighteenth hole was played over Mount Lebanon, in its original site, to the present eighteenth green so that the players crossed one another.

Great structural changes had taken place by 1906 when the new Ladies/Relief course of nine holes was opened for play. The first hole of the Old course was now a short hole in which the tee shot was played over the sandy waste of Mount Lebanon to the green beyond, a distance of 216 yards. Bunkers on developing seaside links of that period were often large, un-raked sandy wastes with clumps of bent grass growing in them. The second, third and fourth holes had been reconstructed and absorbed into the new nine-hole course and the new second hole for the Old course was now played to the Cup green. The sixth and seventh holes in the original lay-out were now combined to form the present third hole with its original plateau green. The bunker on the right of this green is referred to more than once in the minutes as "Joyce Wethered's bunker", but no explanation is anywhere offered for this. In the early descriptions of competitions the bunker on the left below the eighteenth green, appropriately named "Hell", is frequently called "Pandy" (Pandemonium) after the bunker of that name at Musselburgh, but in time the name was dropped.

The lengthening of holes continued over many years and much thought and time was devoted to the possible amalgamation of the tenth and eleventh holes into one long hole. In the end of the day the green of the eleventh hole was carried over the second ditch to its present position and a new tee for the twelfth hole was constructed on the same side of the ditch. The fourteenth hole was greatly lengthened by building a new green in the dunes, and the old green with its filled-in bunkers, just over the Cooper ditch, is clearly identifiable today.

Long before the First World War the Council of the golf club was

123

giving serious consideration to the building of a second eighteen hole course because of the great congestion on the links in the summer months. The subject came up repeatedly and Alexander Grant in 1920 offered the handsome sum of three thousand pounds, free of interest for ten years, to be used for the express purpose of getting another eighteen holes. It was not until 2nd February 1970 that the project finally got off the ground with the formation of a Course development committee under the active chairmanship of Farquhar Thomson. The committee quickly agreed that plans should be laid for the development of a second eighteen hole course incorporating the nine hole Relief course and utilising existing undeveloped ground.

At the 1967 annual general meeting the members were informed that Altyre estates were prepared to sell to the golf club all the ground from the Cooper ditch west to the boundaries of the Covesea caravan site. The Council's intention to buy the land for a sum of £3500 was fully supported, but unfortunately, due to delay on the part of the golf club, the offer was withdrawn by Altyre estates. In 1969 the Covesea development company's offer to purchase the club's lease of this land was rejected since it would prevent any future extension of golfing facilities. The club's determination to extend the golf course was strengthened by the report of the Moray and Nairn coastal policy survey of 1970 in which it was stated that "every encouragement should be given to the proposal [by the Council of the golf club] to provide two eighteen hole golf courses".

Bryan Pennington on the 12th tee of the New Course

The late [Sir] Henry Cotton was called in as golf course architect and visited Lossiemouth on 8th July 1970 to survey the ground and draw up plans for the second course. The plans were implemented under the supervision of A.F. Swan, consultant golf course engineer and a close colleague of Henry Cotton's, but Cotton's recommendation of two starts at the clubhouse was abandoned as it would mean losing the famous eighteenth hole of the Old course. The estimated cost was in the region of £22,800 and this was to be raised from various interested bodies along with a levy on members of the golf club. The largest special general meeting in the history of the club was held in the Lossiemouth town hall on 15th May 1971 with an attendance of 247 members and all the proposals were approved of by 183 votes to 64.

Some idea of the size of the undertaking, and the courage required by the Council of the day, — spurred on by Farquhar Thomson and his New course development committee — can be appreciated when one considers that the land to be turned into a golf course was covered by a large area of high, dense whins. The fairways, tees and greens were marked out and the whins were sprayed with a chemical compound in July 1971. Within twelve months the dead whins were ready for removal and teams of volunteers were recruited to remove roots and stones and to weed and tend the emergent fairways and greens. The droughts of the 1970's caused problems with many of the fairways on the Old course and this slowed down the progress of the work on the New course.

The dedication and single-mindedness of Farquhar Thomson, James Campbell, James Mackenzie the professional, Sandy Edwards and Dr Grace Smith among others was fully rewarded when Farquhar Thomson was invited to open the New eighteen hole course by striking off the first ball on 22nd September 1979 in the presence of an enthusiastic gathering of members. This event opened up a new chapter in the history of the Moray Golf Club.

Farquhar Thomson opens the New Course

125

EPILOGUE

Gentlemen in stiff shirts with dinner-jacket and black tie, accompanied by their ladies in long dresses, no longer stroll over to the Moray Golf Clubhouse on a summer evening after dinner in the Stotfield or Marine Hotels while the inhabitants of Lossiemouth look on in wonder. Those days are long gone and the golf club is a more democratic institution. But while they threw out Ramsay MacDonald because they did not like his politics, these men were responsible for shaping and nurturing the golf links at Stotfield of which the present members are the inheritors.

The well-managed Moray Golf Club of today is in excellent shape to look forward to the next hundred years. The enthusiastic membership, as in the past, plays golf from dawn to dusk both summer and winter, and the courses can accommodate a regular flow of visitors and temporary members with ease. But Lossiemouth has partly lost its way as a holiday resort and its attractions need to be advertised. Charles McKean put it in a nutshell when he wrote — "The town is now looking rather battened down. It needs to face and overcome the challenge presented by the lure of warmer, cheaper climes. The beaches are still splendid." Had he been a golfer as well as an architect and author he would certainly have remarked on the quality of the Old course and the delight of the New course with its aptly christened "Bermuda Triangle".

The Elgin Courant in its literary notice in 1889 on *Letters on Golf* by the first captain asks "Who, that has felt the spring of the turf and enjoyed the rapture of the soaring ball, will not respond to the captain's song?" —

> Wasters, wasters why sit here
> Boozing over Lager beer?
> Sure it's goff you fellows need instead of drinks.
> See that both of you begin
> Ere the gold is off the whin;
> I shall look for you tomorrow on the links.

Those of us who are fortunate enough will be on the links whenever opportunity arises, and above all else, the simple happy things which Lossie offers will always be there. The sound of larks singing overhead in the stillness of a summer morning, the magic of cloud effects and sunshine, the champagne air, the ever-changing sea, and the sense and beauty of spacious surroundings. The charm of the links — and by no means least — the voices and faces of friends. And at the end of the day the sublime joy of quietly telling those friends that you have beaten B.P..

APPENDIX

Captains of the Moray Golf Club

1889-90 Prof. Alex. Lawson
1890-91 Dr G.H.Mackay
1891-92 John MacLeod H.M.I.S.
1892-93 John Rodger
1893-94 W.M.MacBey
1894-95 Wm.Christie
1895-96 James McIsaac
1896-97 F.W.Gibb
1897-98 R.B.Gordon
1898-99 D.Cameron
1899-01 Dr John Taylor
1901-02 John MacLeod H.M.I.S.
1902-04 John B. Mair M.V.O.
1904-05 John Sim
1905-07 John F.Cumming
1907-09 Sheriff J.G.Webster
1909-11 Col.C.J.Johnston
1911-13 J.H.Hair
1913-15 R.I.Cameron
1915-17 John Foster
1917-19 J.M.Fraser
1919-22 John F.Cumming
1922-24 S.McCall Smith
1924-27 A.Low Mustard W.S.
1927-29 Dr G.Smith Sowden
1929-31 J.D.Taylor
1931-33 J.Watson McIsaac W.S.
1933-35 Sir A.P.Gordon Cumming Bt.

1935-38 Col. J.E.Tennant D.S.O.
1938-39 Capt.P.Kynoch Shand
1939-45 S.Gordon MacBey
1946   Sheriff Hamilton Grierson
1947-48 M.G.Stuart
1948-50 Major G.B.Anderson M.C.
1950-52 Dr J.C.Jessop
1952-54 Wm.Christie Jr.
1955-57 R.G.Tulloch
1957   G.B.Cursiter
1957-59 John Stewart
1959-61 A.M.Mackenzie
1961-63 Major I.M.Matheson
1963-65 S.J.Edwards
1965-67 W.Farquhar Thomson
1967-69 Major I.M.Matheson
1969-71 James Campbell
1971-72 Innes Macdonald
1973-74 Dr G.D.Gormley
1975-76 E.K.Christie
1977-78 W.Farquhar Thomson
1979-80 James Stephen
1981-82 R.A.Conti
1983-84 John Harris
1985-86 Dr J.A.McConachie
1987-88 P.N.O'Brien
1989-   W.Farquhar Thomson

The Club Championship

In 1904 the Council decided to procure a cup for scratch play, the cost not to exceed five guineas. The original conditions specified two rounds of the course medal play, the lowest aggregate to win. For many years now the Club Championship has been decided over four rounds medal play.

1904 H.C.Bennett
1905 J.H.Peebles Jr.
1906 G.R.Thomson
1907 G.R.Thomson
1908 G.R.Thomson
1909 G.R.Thomson
1910 G.R.Thomson
1911 G.R.Thomson
1912 W.Christie Jr.
1913 W.Christie Jr.
1914 G.R.Thomson
1915-19 War Years
1920 G.R.Thomson
1921 R.Corstorphine
1922 A.G.Campbell
1923 G.R.Thomson
1924 G.R.Thomson
1925 J.L.Laing
1926 G.R.Thomson
1927 J.L.Laing
1928 H.Ronald
1929 J.H.Peebles
1930 H.Ronald
1931 H.Ronald
1932 G.Wood
1933 G.Wood

1934 G.Wood
1935 G.Wood
1936 Dr J.C.Jessop
1937 G.Wood
1938 Dr J.C.Jessop
1939 G.T.Murray
1940-45 War Years
1946 G.Wood
1947 R.K.Allen
1948 G.Wood
1949 D.M.Cowper
1950 Dr J.Bain
1951 I.M.Matheson
1952 D.M.Cowper
1953 W.J.Stewart
1954 W.J.Stewart
1955 G.B.Cursiter
1956 W.J.Stewart
1957 W.J.Stewart
1958 I.Rodger
1959 W.F.Thomson
1960 C.J.MacLeod
1961 W.F.Thomson
1962 C.J.MacLeod
1963 W.F.Thomson

1964 W.F.Thomson
1965 A.Thomson
1966 N.S.Grant
1967 A.Thomson
1968 N.S.Grant
1969 J.Marnoch
1970 N.S.Grant
1971 R.J.Templeton
1972 A.Thomson
1973 A.Thomson
1974 N.S.Grant
1975 N.S.Grant
1976 N.S.Grant
1977 N.S.Grant
1978 N.S.Grant
1979 N.S.Grant
1980 M.Wilson
1981 M.Wilson
1982 N.S.Grant
1983 M.Wilson
1984 N.S.Grant
1985 N.S.Grant
1986 N.S.Grant
1987 N.S.Grant
1988 I.J.McKenzie

127

The Moray Open Amateur Tournament instituted in 1894

Winners	Runners-Up
1894 L.W.Macpherson (Baberton)	John Sutherland (Dornoch)
1895 A.J.T.Allan (Watsonians)	L.W.Macpherson (Baberton)
1896 J.McCulloch (Aberdeen)	Duncan MacLaren (Mortonhall)
1897 L.W.Macpherson (Baberton)	Duncan MacLaren (Mortonhall)
1898 L.W.Macpherson (Baberton)	A.Cooper (Aberdeen Victoria)
1899 J.W.Wharton Duff (The Hon.Company)	J.G.Stewart (Carnoustie)
1900 J.Ogilvie Kemp (Mortonhall)	I.C.MacGregor (Nairn)
1901 W.D.Davidson (Aberdeen)	A.G.Thomson (Edinburgh Academicals)
1902 J.J.Gillespie (Mortonhall)	J.H.Peebles (Clifton Downs)
1903 J.Gordon Simpson (St Andrews Univ.)	J.A.Donaldson (Aberdeen Bon-Accord)
1904 Robert Harris (Carnoustie)	Captain A.Chalmers (Royal Aberdeen)
1905 Clive Lawrence (Nairn)	C.A.Macpherson (Mortonhall)
1906 F.H.Scroggie (Carnoustie)	W.C.White (Lundin Links)
1907 Gordon Lockhart (Prestwick St Nicholas)	R.Gelletly Jr. (Greenhill)
1908 Gordon Lockhart (Prestwick St Nicholas)	Dr Marshall (Hamilton)
1909 Donald Grant (Royal Dornoch)	Lieut. W.D.Allan (Moray)
1910 Ian Munro (Strathpeffer)	Donald Grant (Royal Dornoch)
1911 C.E.Dick (Royal Dornoch)	G.R.Thomson (Moray)
1912 A.Guthrie Harvey (Nairn)	H.Kingsley Brown (Mortonhall)
1913 G.R.Thomson (Moray)	A.Cooper Jr. (Deeside)

Winners	Runners-up
1914 G.C.Manford (Edinburgh University)	W.C.White (Mortonhall)
1915-19 No Tournament during the War	
1920 Captain Kynoch Cumming (Moray)	A.G.Campbell (Moray)
1921 G.C.Manford (Luffness New)	G.R.Thomson (Moray)
1922 G.C.Manford (Luffness New)	G.Seymour Noon (Didsbury)
1923 W.C.White (Mortonhall)	T.H.Osgood (Forres)
1924 A.G.Campbell (Moray)	W.Willis Mackenzie (Mortonhall)
1925 J.T.Bookless (Inverness)	J.G.Rowan (Drumpellier)
1926 J.G.Rowan (Drumpellier)	Neil Paterson (Moray & Sandy Lodge)
1927 John Birnie Jr. (Inverness)	J.L.Laing (Moray)
1928 R.Stirling (Bishopbriggs)	L.B.Sanderson (Inverness)
1929 George Wilson (Nairn)	P.F.Cameron (Forres)
1930 Hugo Ronald (Moray)	George Wilson (Nairn)
1931 H.McMaster (Old Ranfurly)	A.McKenzie (Moray)
1932 R.Falconer (Moray)	W.Donaldson (New Galloway)
1933 R.S.Walker (Aberdeen University)	Donald Cameron (Kirkintilloch)
1934 Dr J.C.Jessop (Moray)	J.G.Rowan (Hayston)
1935 R.S.Walker (Deeside)	Donald Cameron (Kirkintilloch)
1936 Dr J.C.Jessop (Moray)	D.C.Leith Buchanan (Nairn)
1937 R.S.Walker (Deeside)	H.G.Mackintosh (Royal Aberdeen)
1938 K.B.Murray (Eastwood)	J.S.Montgomerie (Cambuslang)
1939 Dr J.C.Jessop (Moray)	A.M.W.Coburn (Aberdeen University)
1940-46 No Tournament during the War	
1947 G.T.Murray (Moray)	A.J.D.Blaikie (Royal Musselburgh)
1948 W.D.Campbell (Moray)	B.W.Wilken (Elgin)
1949 Dr J.C.Jessop (Moray)	A.Kinnaird (Moray)
1950 J.Paterson (Spey Bay)	G.T.Murray (Moray)
1951 W.D.Campbell (Moray)	Dr H.N.M.Thomson (Elgin)
1952 A.Cordiner (Murcar)	J.Lindsay (Falkirk Tryst)
1953 J.Lindsay (Falkirk Tryst)	I.P.A.Rodger (Moray)
1954 D.F.Beatson (Kingsknowe)	C.J.MacLeod (Moray)
1955 J.Paterson (Buckpool)	E.B.Robinson (Moray)
1956 E.B.Robinson (Moray)	W.J.Stewart (Moray)
1957 W.Hector (Buckpool)	A.S.E.Dale (Baberton)
1958 A.W.How (Moray)	W.Hector (Buckpool)
1959 C.J.MacLeod (Moray)	S.F.Smith (Moray)
1960 J.Ross Anderson (Moray)	J.Shannon (Cawder)
1961 C.J.MacLeod (Moray)	R.M.Grant (Elgin)
1962 W.F.Thomson (Moray)	J.Marnoch (Garmouth)
1963 I.P.A.Rodger (Elgin)	J.Morrison (Moray)
1964 W.Reid (Moray)	W.F.Thomson (Moray)
1965 N.S.Grant (Elgin)	R.M.Grant (Hazlehead)
1966 A.Thomson (Moray)	I.P.A.Rodger (Moray)
1967 N.S.Grant (Elgin)	R.J.Gray (Prestonfield)
1968 R.J.Gray (Prestonfield)	I.P.A.Rodger (Elgin)
1969 N.S.Grant (Moray)	W.F.Thomson (Moray)
1970 A.Thomson (Moray)	A.P.Thomson (Inverness)
1971 R.M.Grant (Aberdeen Caledonian)	N.S.Grant (Moray)
1972 J.Farquhar (Strathlene)	N.S.Grant (Moray)
1973 N.S.Grant (Moray)	P.G.Buchanan (Williamwood)
1974 A.Thomson (Moray)	N.S.Grant (Moray)
1975 I.G. Taylor (Moray)	B.Pennington (Moray)
1976 R.M.Grant (Aberdeen Caledonian)	I.Imray (Moray)
1977 H.B.Stuart (Moray)	B.Cramb (Moray)
1978 H.B.Stuart (Moray)	F.G.Mathers (Moray)
1979 I.D.McIntosh (Moray)	I.G.Taylor (Elgin)
1980 N.S.Grant (Moray)	M.Wilson (Moray)
1981 M.Wilson (Moray)	C.J.MacLeod (Moray)
1982 M.Wilson (Moray)	R.M.Grant (Aberdeen Caledonian)
1983 A.D.Nichols (Eaton)	N.S.Grant (Moray)
1984 J.A.Scott (Murcar)	C.J.MacLeod (Moray)
1985 M.Cattanach (Garmouth)	J.McCallum (Moray)
1986 R.H.Willox (Deeside)	N.S.Grant (Moray)
1987 G.A.Moir (Fraserburgh)	R.D.Morrison (Moray)
1988 I.D.McIntosh (Moray)	N.Robson (Elgin)

The Lady Gordon Cumming Cup

The cup was presented in 1892 by Lady Gordon Cumming of Gordonstoun and Altyre. She was Florence Garner, daughter of William Garner who was Commodore of the New York Yacht Club, and her parents were drowned within sight of their Staten Island home when she was four years of age. The conditions of play for this cup are unusual — the higher handicap player starts the match a number of holes up, which is equal to half the difference in the handicaps.

1892 A.Peterkin	1924 C.J.Doig	1959 Dr J.A.McConachie
1893 J.McIsaac	1925 F.A.MacBeth	1960 P.Stewart
1894 J.McIsaac	1926 F.A.MacBeth	1961 J.McKenzie
1895 D.Cameron	1927 F.A.MacBeth	1962 W.J.Stewart
1896 W.Christie	1928 H.Ronald	1963 J.Morrison
1897 J.McIsaac	1929 G.Wood	1964 J.Cock
1898 W.Macdonald	1930 I.C.Cumming	1965 I.M.Matheson
1899 R.A.B.Coull	1931 W.Stewart	1966 N.S.Grant
1900 L.Anderson	1932 A.Reid	1967 R.M.Low
1901 J.McIsaac	1933 G.Wood	1968 W.F.Thomson
1902 D.West	1934 G.Wood	1969 H.S.McKenzie
1903 W.Christie Jr.	1935 W.F.Gray	1970 J.Baillie
1904 W.Christie Jr.	1936 R.W.Symon	1971 I.M.Matheson
1905 J.Reid	1937 W.J.Clark	1972 C.E.Bentham
1906 J.A.Cameron	1938 J.M.Gault	1973 D.A.Duncan
1907 J.W.McIsaac	1939 D.Auld	1974 W.S.Wood
1908 G.R.Thomson	1940-45 War Years	1975 N.S.Grant
1909 J.W.McIsaac	1946 Dr H.M.Tucker	1976 W.F.Thomson
1910 G.J.McLay	1947 J.E.Souter	1977 R.Bell
1911 A.G.Campbell	1948 J.Stewart	1978 S.Mitchell
1912 G.J.McLay	1949 Lt.D.Mitchell	1979 J.F.Perrie
1913 G.R.Thomson	1950 J.L.Stewart	1980 J.B.Thomson
1914 A.G.Campbell	1951 W.C.Edwards	1981 A.Stewart
1915 A.G.Campbell	1952 R.B.Calder	1982 W.MacDonald
1916-18 War Years	1953 C.J.MacLeod	1983 C.J.MacLeod
1919 A.G.Campbell	1954 J.Crockett	1984 W.Stewart
1920 A.G.Campbell	1955 J.F.Mitchell	1985 A.S.Garden
1921 F.A.MacBeth	1956 I.M.Matheson	1986 A.Cowie
1922 F.A.MacBeth	1957 A.Campbell	1987 C.D.Stewart
1923 F.A.MacBeth	1958 J.B.Stewart	1988 I.Goldie

The Jubilee Challenge Cup

The cup was presented on 6th May 1935 by the captain, Lt.Colonel J.E. Tennant, D.S.O., M.C., of Innes House, to commemorate the Silver Jubilee of King George V. The cup is open to ladies and gentlemen and is for the lowest medal round under handicap. Miss Chrystal MacGeagh in 1950 is the only lady to win it so far.

1935 Joseph Baikie	1957 D.Laing	1973 A.Macdonald
1936 Joseph Baikie	1958 E.M.Stewart	1974 R.Stradling
1937 George Wood	1959 A.Grant	1975 M.G.Clarke
1938 Dr J.C.Jessop	1960 C.Tough	1976 J.Edwards
1939 D.S.Laing	1961 D.M.Rattray	1977 J.C.Boyd
1940-45 War Years	1962 J.G.S.Crombie	1978 P.J.Chambers
1946 G.T.Murray	1963 R.A.Conti	1979 D.E.Caldwell
1947 John Crockett	1964 W.G.Calder	1980 R.Owen
1948 John Stewart	1965 P.Stewart	1981 W.Stewart
1949 E.Meldrum	1966 J.C.Thomson	1982 M.Wilson
1950 Miss C.MacGeagh	1967 J.H.Stark	1983 E.T.Fiske
1951 J.Souter	1968 J.C.Thomson	1984 P.Stewart
1952 W.B.Souter	1969 D.J.Reardon	1985 W.Johnston
1953 Cdr.J.R.J.Cowlin	1970 E.D.Dodson	1986 T.Mackie
1954 A.E.Davies	1971 J.Edwards	1987 M.G.Young
1955 J.W.C.Thomson	1972 K.Anderson	1988 A.McK.Campbell
1956 W.Crockett		

The Gordon Prize

This most unusual cup was presented in 1897 by the Hon. John E. Gordon who was the Member of Parliament for Morayshire. The names of the winners are engraved on the bosses of the cup which has no plinth.

1897 W.Christie	1928 Hugo Ronald	1961 C.J.MacLeod
1898 W.Christie Jr.	1929 George Wood	1962 C.J.MacLeod
1899 John Hunter	1930 O.W.Milne	1963 R.A.Page
1900 W.Christie Jr.	1931 Hugo Ronald	1964 J.Morrison
1901 G.Bennett	1932 K.Mackessack	1965 D.Dean
1902 J.Mackenzie Forbes	1933 G.R.Thomson	1966 C.D.Stewart
1903 E.Kintrea	1934 W.A.McCulloch	1967 P.Stewart
1904 A.J.Ferguson	1935 Hugo Ronald	1968 W.F.Thomson
1905 J.G.Cattell	1936 D.G.Hughes	1969 J.J.Smith
1906 G.R.Thomson	1937 A.Campbell	1970 W.F.Thomson
1907 J.A.Cameron	1938 L.S.Meikle	1971 M.Wilson
1908 G.R.Thomson	1939 G.T.Murray	1972 W.F.Thomson
1909 G.R.Thomson	1940-45 War Years	1973 J.F.Perrie
1910 J.F.Cumming	1946 W.A.Mackie	1974 C.D.Stewart
1911 J.F.Cumming	1947 W.J.Stewart	1975 M.Wilson
1912 W.Christie Jr.	1948 W.J.Stewart	1976 M.S.Campbell
1913 Alec Macdonald	1949 W.J.Stewart	1977 C.D.Stewart
1914 W.Christie Jr.	1950 I.M.Matheson	1978 I.D.McIntosh
1915 James Welsh	1951 John Stewart	1979 J.Slater
1916-19 European War	1952 W.B.Souter	1980 I.S.Pirie
1920 G.R.Thomson	1953 W.F.Thomson	1981 I.J.McKenzie
1921 W.Campbell	1954 R.G.Tulloch	1982 W.F.Thomson
1922 F.A.MacBeth	1955 W.Petrie	1983 C.J.MacLeod
1923 A.G.Campbell	1956 I.M.Matheson	1984 G.J.Abel
1924 T.H.Lawson	1957 J.B.Stewart	1985 A.Finlay
1925 A.Low Mustard	1958 J.Campbell	1986 L.G.Jaffray
1926 R.Falconer	1959 A.Grant	1987 G.Devine
1927 R.A.Frame	1960 I.M.Matheson	1988 C.Sandison

The R.Innes Cameron Cup

Presented in June 1908 by R.Innes Cameron of Elgin, captain in 1913-15. R.I.Cameron was a distiller and broker, and the sole proprietor of The Teaninich Distillery, Alness, Ross-shire. The cup, value ten guineas, to be played for annually by players with handicaps of nine and over.

1908 J.G.Reid	1935 J.Baikie	1965 W.T.Fiske
1909 J.Welsh	1936 A.M.Mackenzie	1966 D.Dean
1910 D.T.Smith	1937 G.T.Murray	1967 A.Flett
1911 T.H.Lawson	1938 F.Gault	1968 L.P.Thomas
1912 J.Welsh	1939 A.Farquhar	1969 R.A.Conti
1913 C.J.Doig	1940-45 War Years	1970 A.G.Imray
1914 A.T.Welsh	1946 J.Crockett	1971 P.Griffiths
1915 R.Macpherson	1947 J.Inkson	1972 W.Thomson
1916-18 War Years	1948 A.Grant	1973 F.Clunas
1919 J.H.Lee	1949 J.Stewart	1974 I.J.McKenzie
1920 D.Skinner Jr.	1950 M.S.Campbell	1975 I.S.Pirie
1921 C.M.Johnston	1951 J.Stewart	1976 N.B.G.MacLeod
1922 J.Foster	1952 G.F.Murray	1977 A.B.Cave
1923 Major Powell	1953 C.J.MacLeod	1978 J.Souter
1924 J.S.Masson	1954 G.King	1979 P.Devine
1925 A.Tocher	1955 J.Skinner	1980 W.Youngson
1926 W.Stewart	1956 J.B.Souter	1981 W.MacDonald
1927 A.MacDougall	1957 J.Campbell	1982 W.M.Simpson
1928 W.J.McCulloch	1958 G.King	1983 J.B.McIntyre
1929 A.Reid	1959 M.S.Campbell	1984 K.Cordukes
1930 W.A.McCulloch	1960 G.Thomson	1985 D.Fisher
1931 A.McKenzie	1961 C.Thomson	1986 J.Petrie
1932 P.C.Knight	1962 G.Thomson	1987 D.McGrath
1933 G.Horne Jr.	1963 A.J.Milne	1988 J.McGrath
1934 A.Campbell	1964 W.McBride	

The Cumming Cup

The silver cup on an elegant silver stand was presented by J.F. Cumming in 1903 for the annual winners of the monthly medal. However, since 1924 the cup has been awarded for the best score under handicap at the Autumn Meeting. John Fleetwood Cumming of Cardhu Distillery was captain from 1905-1907 and again from 1919-1922.

1904 J.G.Cattell	1933 R.W.Souter	1964 C.Thomson
1905 W.Christie Jr.	1934 W.A.McCulloch	1965 J.M.Cameron
1906 Capt.C.P.Doig	1935 F.Harland	1966 N.A.McConachie
1907 G.R.Thomson	1936 T.K.Denny	1967 J.C.MacLean
1908 J.W.McIsaac	1937 P.A.P.Mackenzie	1968 D.Hardie
1909 G.J.McLay	1938 W.S.Harris	1969 K.McKenzie
1910 Dr Jenkins	1939 A.Farquhar	1970 J.A.B.Little
1911 G.R.Thomson	1940-45 War Years	1971 J.Slater
1912 John Macdonald	1946 A.Kinnaird	1972 R.Sandison
1913 James Welsh	1947 J.C.Thomson	1973 J.White
1914 James Falconer	1948 A.Reid	1974 C.E.Bentham
1915 J.H.Lee	1949 R.B.Calder	1975 J.D.Garden
1916-19 European War	1950 W.Mitchell	1976 M.S.Campbell
1920 A.Low Mustard	1951 J.B.Brown	1977 J.Crockett
1921 H.Ronald	1952 G.Stewart	1978 W.F.Thomson
1922 G.R.Thomson	1953 C.G.R.Manson	1979 J.Slater
1923 G.R.Thomson	1954 J.McKinlay	1980 D.M.Rattray
1924 D.Mackessack	1955 G.Robertson	1981 J.W.Souter
1925 J.Macdonald	1956 D.Mitchell	1982 W.MacDonald
1926 Ian McCulloch	1957 W.Cowie	1983 J.Jordan
1927 H.Ronald	1958 J.McLeod	1984 D.J.Flett
1928 A.J.McCaskie	1959 J.C.Thomson	1985 A.Fiske
1929 H.R.Spence	1960 J.McLeod	1986 J.M.Campbell
1930 Col.R.D.Crawford	1961 J.Stewart	1987 M.Cross
1931 A.McKenzie	1962 P.F.Smith	1988 M.J.Madden
1932 R.H.Gray	1963 W.T.Fiske	

The Veterans Shield

This handsome shield was presented in 1921 by Sir Alexander Grigor Jeans of Liverpool, one of the original members, whose father was the proprietor of the old *Elgin Courier*. It is competed for annually by match play among members aged fifty-five years and over. The shield carries the inscription — "Our nature here is not unlike our wine, Some sorts when old continue brisk and fine".

1921 R.J.Wilson	1949 A.F.H.Grierson	1969 J.Stewart
1922 Rev.W.E.Shaw	1950 Dr J.C.Jessop.	1970 G.Wood
1923 J.F.Cumming	1951 F.C.Thomson	1971 D.Laing
1924 J.F.Cumming	1952 Dr J.C.Jessop	1972 I.M.Matheson
1925 J.F.Cumming	1953 Dr J.C.Jessop	1973 W.P.Cumming
1926 P.Lamming	1954 D.Stewart	1974 D.Auld
1927 W.Campbell	1955 A.M.Mackenzie	1975 G.Wood
1928 J.F.Cumming	1956 M.Reid	1976 J.McLeod
1929 Sir A.R.Murray	1957 D.Stewart	1977 D.Hardy
1930 J.H.Fyfe	1958 E.Meldrum	1978 A.D.Calder
1931 Sir A.R.Murray	1959 E.Meldrum	1979 J.G.Laing
1932 A.M.Fairbairn	1960 E.Meldrum	1980 J.E.Souter
1933 Dr J.Anderson	1961 J.F.Mitchell	1981 J.S.Denholm
1934 Dr J.Anderson	1962 J.F.Mitchell	1982 J.S.Denholm
1935 J.McDonald	1963 J.F.Mitchell	1983 D.Auld
1936 G.Turnbull	1964 D.Gault	1984 J.A.Fordyce
1937 Col.H.L.Warden	1965 J.C.Thomson	1985 D.Auld
1938 A.F.H.Grierson	1966 R.M.Low	1986 A.M.Curle
1939-46 War Years	1967 D.Auld	1987 A.Flett
1948 Dr J.C.Jessop	1968 D.M.Cowper	1988 W.A.Brown

The Victory Foursome Cup

Presented by H.W.Morrison, Marine Hotel, Lossiemouth, (a London member) in October 1919. The cup, value £20, was to be played for as the Council decided, and Mr Morrison offered to present a replica to the winner each year. This was the beginning of the very popular Victory foursomes which are decided by matchplay.

1920 Capt. Wakelin & S.Morrison	1958 D.M.Cowper & C.J.MacLeod
1921 W.Campbell & Major Welsh	1959 A.Stewart & P.G.Little
1922 A.G.Mackay & J.H.Perry	1960 J.B.Stewart & J.Cock
1923 J.H.Perry & B.Hopps	1961 T.Wilson & J.M.Campbell
1924 H.Ronald & Rev. J.Niven	1962 C.Thomson & J.W.C.Thomson
1925 D.W.Johnston & J.Harthill	1963 A.McLeod & P.Stewart
1926 R.Falconer & W.Stewart	1964 W.B.Souter & W.Simpson
1927 J.L.Hamilton & N.Johnston	1965 I.M.Matheson & J.F.Mitchell
1928 G.Wood & W.Alexander	1966 D.M.Cowper & L.McIntosh
1929 Col.J.E.Tennant & G.MacLeod	1967 W.Reid & J.G.Mackay
1930 E.G.Hay & T.K.Denny	1968 I.Rodger & N.S.Stewart
1931 H.Ronald & G.P.C.Anderson	1969 A.J.Souter & P.Stewart
1932 R.Falconer & A.M.Anderson	1970 J.C.Conboy & R.A.Page
1933 G.Wood & S.G.MacBey	1971 A.D.Calder & A.G.Calder
1934 W.J.Clark & P.Turnbull	1972 C.Thomson & J.W.C.Thomson
1935 J.Macdonald & R.Grigor	1973 J.Jordan & A.Anderson
1936 A.G.Murray & W.D.Campbell	1974 R.A.Page & J.C.MacLean
1937 W.S.Harris & S.Drysdale	1975 B.Cramb & C.E.Smith
1938 H.W.Urquhart & W.S.Harris	1976 R.A.Conti & A.E.Davies
1939 H.Ronald & Sir J.Donald	1977 I.J.McKenzie & A.Cowie
1940-46 War Years	1978 M.M.Macleman & L.G.Jaffray
1948 A.M.Alexander & J.Stewart	1979 S.Mitchell & A.J.Stephen
1949 W.Cowie & John Stewart	1980 J.J.Smith & C.D.Stewart
1950 W.C.Edwards & C.Thomson	1981 C.J.MacLeod & I.S.Pirie
1951 M.S.Campbell & W.Thomson	1982 G.J.Abel & H.B.Stuart
1952 W.J.Stewart & J.W.C.Thomson	1983 W.A.Smith & K.G.Armit
1953 G.F.Murray & W.Robertson	1984 C.J.MacLeod & J.S.MacPherson
1954 J.E.Souter & J.W.C.Thomson	1985 K.G.Armit & W.A.Smith
1955 W.Robertson & J.Laing	1986 J.M.Campbell & W.C.Youngson
1956 W.J.Stewart & A.Grant	1987 A.Fiske & W.T.Fiske
1957 W.J.Stewart & D.Laing	1988 T.J.Smith & I. Goldie

The Pitgaveny Gold Medal

The gold medal was presented by Captain James Brander Dunbar of Pitgaveny on 1st January 1924 and is awarded for the best scratch score at the Autumn Meeting.

1924 F.A.MacBeth	1949 J.Souter	1969 J.A.B.Little
1925 A.Low Mustard	1950 W.D.Campbell	1970 A.Thomson
1926 G.B.Crole	1951 D.M.Cowper	1971 W.F.Thomson
1927 J.L.Laing	1952 Lt.W.R.Hunter	1972 R.A.Page
1928 G.B.Crole	1953 A.Kinnaird	1973 L.G.Jaffray
1929 H.Ronald	1954 R.B.Calder	1974 B.Cramb
1930 H.Ronald	1955 H.S.McKenzie	1975 W.F.Thomson
1931 H.Ronald	1956 W.G.Howell	1976 B.Cramb
1932 S.Smith	1957 G.Wood	1977 I.J.McKenzie
1933 W.J.Clark	1958 A.Kinnaird	1978 M.Wilson
1934 G.Wood	1959 J.C.Thomson	1979 N.S.Grant
1935 G.Wood	1960 S.J.Edwards	1980 L.G.Jaffray
1936 G.Wood	1961 D.J.McDonald	1981 N.S.Grant
1937 Dr J.C.Jessop	1962 D.M.Cowper	1982 K.G.Armit
1938 H.Ronald	1963 J.M.Campbell	1983 N.S.Grant
1939 W.S.Harris	1964 W.F.Thomson	1984 M.Wilson
1940-45 War Years	1965 A.Thomson	1985 C.J.MacLeod
1946 G.T.Murray	1966 A.Thomson	1986 N.S.Grant
1947 Dr J.C.Jessop	1967 L.P.Thomas	1987 C.J.MacLeod
1948 W.D.Campbell	1968 J.Marnoch	1988 I.J.McKenzie

The Spring Meeting

The competition began in 1924 and a new trophy for the matchplay stages was presented by John Harris, captain 1983-84.

1924 J.Watson McIsaac	1949 J.Crockett	1969 J.C.MacLean
1925 G.R.Thomson	1950 W.J.Stewart	1970 W.Crockett
1926 J.A.Cattell	1951 W.A.Youngson	1971 H.Flett
1927 H.Smith	1952 G.F.Murray	1972 J.C.Lawrence
1928 W.J.Macdonald	1953 L.Munro	1973 L.G.Jaffray
1929 R.Falconer	1954 J.C.Thomson	1974 D.Hardy
1930 C.P.R.Johnston	1955 E.B.Robinson	1975 W.C.Youngson
1931 H.R.Spence	1956 I.M.Matheson	1976 A.G.Imray
1932 A.E.S.Reid	1957 W.J.Stewart	1977 D.Hardy
1933 Dr J.C.Jessop	1958 C.Tough	1978 K.Williams
1934 D.Mackessack	1959 J.F.Mitchell	1979 W.A.Muir
1935 G.Wood	1960 L.McIntosh	1980 I.J.McKenzie
1936 J.C.MacLeod	1961 W.F.Thomson	1981 C.E.Smith
1937 W.J.Stewart	1962 W.J.Stewart	1982 R.Dunbar
1938 W.J.Clark	1963 W.B.Souter	1983 S.Stables
1939 W.Meldrum	1964 R.B.Calder	1984 S.Armstrong
1940-45 War Years	1965 J.W.Taylor	1985 E.B.Souter
1946 G.Thomson	1966 J.A.McConachie	1986 H.A.Kinnaird
1947 J.Crockett	1967 A.Thomson	1987 A.Hepburn
1948 G.Calder	1968 A.Thomson	1988 J.R.Gardiner

The Excalibur Cup

This was presented by Arthur Duthie, wealthy fish salesman and racehorse owner, in 1947. The Council were pleased to agree to the conditions that the cup should be played for annually — one medal round on handicap — by members of the Nairn, Nairn Dunbar, Burghead, Hopeman and Moray Golf Clubs. These clubs represented some of the fishing ports on the Moray Firth with which Arthur Duthie & Co. was involved.

1947 J.Inkson	1961 J.Morrison	1975 A.G.McKenzie
1948 E.Thomson	1962 A.Thomson	1976 J.S.Sim
1949 E.Meldrum	1963 R.Morrison	1977 M.S.Campbell
1950 J.E.Souter	1964 J.Souter	1978 G.Fowler
1951 J.MacKenzie	1965 G.Farquhar	1979 I.Stewart
1952 J.M.Campbell	1966 G.S.Stewart	1980 A.R.Souter
1953 W.F.Thomson	1967 J.Stewart	1981 N.Stewart
1954 I.M.Matheson	1968 I.Thomson	1982 K.Ingram
1955 D.Laing	1969 D.Stolworthy	1983 K.Williams
1956 John Souter	1970 N.A.McConachie	1984 R.Wilson
1957 J.G.Laing	1971 W.Cowie	1985 I.Stewart
1958 A.Thomson	1972 C.E.Bentham	1986 S.Y.Gordon
1959 J.Stewart	1973 M.J.Madden	1987 C.A.Smith
1960 A.Thomson	1974 J.S.Dougan	1988 N.D.Grant

The Innes Matheson Cup

Donated in 1954 by Major I.M. Matheson, T.D., J.P., twice captain of the club. This cup is awarded to the winner of the annual scratch matchplay championship.

1954 A.Kinnaird	1966 A.Thomson	1978 N.S.Grant
1955 W.J.Stewart	1967 W.F.Thomson	1979 M.Wilson
1956 I.Rodger	1968 A.Thomson	1980 G.J.Abel
1957 W.F.Thomson	1969 N.S.Grant	1981 C.J.MacLeod
1958 A.Kinnaird	1970 A.Thomson	1982 S.Macdonald
1959 C.J.MacLeod	1971 N.S.Grant	1983 I.J.McKenzie
1960 W.F.Thomson	1972 N.S.Grant	1984 N.S.Grant
1961 I.M.Matheson	1973 I.D.McIntosh	1985 S.Mitchell
1962 W.F.Thomson	1974 N.S.Grant	1986 G.J.Abel
1963 W.F.Thomson	1975 B.L.Cramb	1987 S.Mitchell
1964 W.F.Thomson	1976 N.S.Grant	1988 W.F.Thomson
1965 A.Thomson	1977 M.Wilson	

The Sam Smith Cup

The trophy was presented by Sam Smith, a former secretary of the golf club, in 1955.

1955 A.E.S.Reid	1968 D.Mitchell	1979 M.P.Farquhar
1956 J.C.Thomson	1969 I.Macdonald	1980 A.R.Thomson
1957 M.S.Campbell	1970 P.Griffiths	1981 I.Sloan
1958 J.F.Lindsay	1971 J.A.McConachie	1982 J.G.Anderson
1961 R.Morrison	1972 R.A.Conti	1983 A.R.Souter
1962 W.S.Scott	1973 J.R.Smith	1984 R.Sheils
1963 A.J.Milne	1974 J.C.MacLean	1985 R.Welldon
1964 A.Flett	1975 J.A.Mitchell	1986 D.Petrie
1965 W.F.Liebnitz	1976 B.Pennington	1987 G.Houston
1966 J.W.Cock	1977 J.A.Gordon	1988 J.J.Smith
1967 J.Marnoch	1978 P.Devine	

The H.P.Stewart Trophy (Asian Cup)

This handsome cup was presented in 1962 by a past secretary of the golf club, H.P.Stewart, who had won it at Calcutta in 1937. Then known as The Asian Golf Challenge Bowl, it was first competed for at Calcutta in 1902.

1962 W.F.Thomson	1971 J.Hamilton	1980 J.F.Perrie
1963 J.W.C.Thomson	1972 J.C.MacLean	1981 C.E.Smith
1964 W.F.Thomson	1973 C.G.Prideaux	1982 A.J.Stephen
1965 R.S.Stewart	1974 A.Thomson	1983 R.A.Page
1966 J.M.McKenzie	1975 A.Thomson	1984 A.M.Curle
1967 C.H.Simpson	1976 D.A.Duncan	1985 W.Stewart
1968 N.A.McConachie	1977 M.Wilson	1986 J.Petrie
1969 J.Marnoch	1978 N.B.G.MacLeod	1987 R.Sheils
1970 I.D.McIntosh	1979 M.Wilson	1988 G.W.Cowper

The Winter Cup

Presented by Major G.Boyd Anderson, M.B.E., M.C., in 1969.

1969-70 R.A.Page	1980-81 P.N.O'Brien
1970-71 J.Slater	1981-82 M.Wilson
1971-72 R.Rothnie	1982-83 C.W.Cleet
1972-73 J.Jordan	1983-84 H.A.Kinnaird
1975-76 D.MacKintosh	1984-85 R.J.Bufton
1976-77 W.P.Cumming	1985-86 J.Rae
1977-78 A.M.Rose	1986-87 R.Wilson
1978-79 P.N.O'Brien	1987-88 R.Daughney
1979-80 W.P.Cumming	

The Par Cup

The cup was presented in 1972 by J.T.Patrick, an Elgin solicitor, for competition by members of the Moray and Nairn Golf Clubs.

1972 R.A.Page	1979 I.S.Pirie	1984 W.Allen
1974 B.D.Fraser (N)	1980 I.J.McKenzie	1985 K.Thomson
1976 N.S.Grant	1981 W.F.Thomson	1986 D.MacKintosh
1977 A.T.Mackenzie	1982 J.W.Souter	1987 A.R.Souter
1978 W.F.Thomson	1983 W.B.Souter	1988 J.R.Gardiner

The Clydesdale Bank Trophy

The silver salver was presented to the club by the Clydesdale Bank in 1979.

1979 H.H.Rourke	1983 C.J.MacLeod	1986 N.S.Grant
1980 M.Wilson	1984 A.J.Stephen	1987 K.G.Armit
1981 N.S.Grant	1985 C.J.MacLeod	1988 I.J.McKenzie
1982 M.Wilson		

The Captain's Prize

Presented by the captain, John Harris, in November 1984.

1983 W.Macleman	1985 D.Scott	1987 A.R.Souter
1984 W.Sandison	1986 A.R.Souter	1988 W.Stewart

The Jim Thom Quaich

James G.Thom, a very respected past secretary of the golf club, presented this trophy in 1979.

1979 J.Smith	1983 I.Taylor	1986 W.Johnston
1980 G.S.Thomson	1984 A.J.Edwards	1987 A.M.Rose
1981 A.R.Thomson	1985 R.D.Grant	1988 G.Hamilton
1982 A.Stewart		

The Ibis Club Challenge Cup

The cup was presented to the club in 1927 "in memory of D.C.B. and G.G.A." It is competed for annually in mixed foursomes by matchplay.

1927 J.Anderson & Miss K.S.Macdonald	1961 J.Stewart & Mrs Hamilton
1928 G.Martineau & Miss Hopps	1962 J.Morrison & Mrs I.Douglas
1929 K.C.Fyfe & Miss Pitcher	1963 W.J.Stewart & Miss M.Cameron
1930 Sir R.MacLean & Mrs G.B.Crole	1964 J.R.Anderson & Mrs Clark
1931 A.McKenzie & Mrs J.McGill	1965 J.A.B.Little & Mrs I.Douglas
1932 K.Mackessack & Miss H.Cameron	1966 L.McIntosh & Mrs E.Saul
1933 S.A.Millington & Miss M.Murray	1967 W.F.Thomson & Miss C.MacGeagh
1934 W.L.Millington & Miss J.Murray	1968 W.B.Souter & Mrs A.Souter
1935 Lt.Cdr.H.C.Maclean & Miss C.MacGeagh	1969 I.M.Matheson & Miss E.Geddes
1936 K.A.S.Morrice & Mrs Morrice	1970 C.D.Stewart & Mrs I.Douglas
1937 G.R.Thomson & Mrs Crawford	1971 I.D.McIntosh & Mrs G.Gormley
1938 T.H.G.Harris & Miss M.McGill	1972 J.M.Duggie & Miss E.Geddes
1939 Dr Pinkerton & Mrs Pinkerton	1973 C.D.Stewart & Mrs I.Douglas
1940-46 War Years	1974 W.B.Souter & Mrs A.Souter
1947 Dr W.J.Lyon Dean & Miss C.MacGeagh	1975 W.B.Souter & Mrs A.Souter
1948 Dr W.J.Lyon Dean & Miss C.MacGeagh	1976 C.D.Stewart & Mrs I.Douglas
1949 A.Kinnaird & Mrs M.Main	1977 N.MacLeod & Mrs E.Rattray
1950 W.L.Robertson & Mrs Robertson	1978 N.S.Grant & Mrs M.Grant
1951 J.O.R.Martin & Miss C.MacGeagh	1979 N.S.Grant & Mrs M.Grant
1952 G.Stewart & Miss B.Chetham	1980 N.S.Grant & Mrs M.Grant
1953 W.Petrie & Miss C.MacGeagh	1981 N.S.Grant & Mrs M.Grant
1954 W.J.Stewart & Mrs Buchanan	1982 A.R.Souter & Miss G.Robertson
1955 C.J.MacLeod & Mrs M.Main	1983 Drs J.A. & J.M.McConachie
1956 J.Stewart & Mrs Hamilton	1984 D.M.Rattray & Mrs E.Rattray
1957 R.B.Calder & Miss M.Cameron	1985 W.F.Thomson & Mrs E.Thomson
1958 A.W.How & Mrs W.Christie	1986 W.A.Smith & Mrs I.Thear
1959 C.J.MacLeod & Mrs W.Christie	1987 N.S.Grant & Mrs M.Grant
1960 L.McIntosh & Mrs M.Main	1988 A.D.Calder & Mrs E.Smith

The N.P.F.A. Challenge Shield

The shield is awarded to the winners of the annual mixed foursomes stroke play competition.

1950 W.A.Mackie & Miss M.Cameron	1970 H.S.McKenzie & Mrs A.Pullar
1951 V.Martin & Mrs Markes	1971 C.D.Stewart & Mrs D.J.Laing
1952 Lt.Hunter & Mrs Matthews	1972 A.E.Davies & Mrs A.Torr
1953 G.Rennie & Miss Fletcher	1974 A.M.Farquhar & Miss E.Geddes
1954 H.P.Stewart & Mrs Buchanan	1975 W.B.Souter & Mrs M.Watt
1955 A.M.Campbell & Mrs A.Weir	1976 W.J.Stewart & Miss B.Malcolmson
1957 D.Laing & Miss I.B.Watt	1977 J.Clark & Mrs E.Rattray
1958 A.W.How & Miss Allan	1978 D.H.Sim & Mrs E.Christie
1960 W.Crockett & Miss Paterson	1979 I.S.Pirie & Mrs M.Souter
1961 W.J.Stewart & Miss Allan	1980 J.S.Denholm & Mrs M.Grant
1962 L.McIntosh & Mrs E.Saul	1981 D.Gormley & Mrs I.Campbell
1963 W.J.Stewart & Mrs A.Pullar	1982 J.Souter & Mrs I.Prideaux
1964 W.J.Stewart & Mrs M.Main	1983 N.S.Grant & Mrs M.Grant
1965 C.D.Stewart & Mrs A.Weir	1984 W.A.Smith & Mrs I.Campbell
1966 L.McIntosh & Mrs I.Douglas	1985 A.Cowie & Mrs A.Torr
1967 L.McIntosh & Mrs M.McIntosh	1986 K.S.Wares & Mrs J.Tulloch
1968 J.Stewart & Miss Allan	1987 A.M.Curle & Miss B.Malcolmson
1969 C.D.Stewart & Mrs Oulton	1988 K.S.Wares & Mrs I.Thear

The Sheriff Webster Cup

The handsome trophy was presented in 1903 by Sheriff James G. Webster who was captain in 1907-09. It is awarded to the annual winner of the Ladies' club championship and is decided by four rounds medal play.

1903 Elma Stuart	1931 H.C.Cameron	1963 B.Chetham
1904 Bertha Mitchell	1932 H.C.Cameron	1964 C.MacGeagh
1905 I.M.Webster	1933 Mrs H.C.Marr	1965 Mrs M.Main
1906 M.H.Benton	1934 J.E.Tomes	1966 B.Chetham
1907 M.H.Benton	1935 C.M.Nicolson	1967 I.Douglas
1908 M.H.Benton	1936 W.Drysdale	1968 C.MacGeagh
1909 Isobel Webster	1937 W.Drysdale	1969 Mrs M.Main
1910 M.H.Benton	1938 M.McGill	1970 E.Geddes
1911 M.H.Benton	1939 M.McGill	1971 E.Geddes
1912 Mrs Willock-Pollen	1940-46 War Years	1972 E.Geddes
1913 G.M.Ford	1947 C.MacGeagh	1973 G.Smith
1914 E.E.Helme	1948 C.MacGeagh	1974 E.Geddes
1915 H.McIsaac	1949 Mrs M.Main	1975 B.Cramb
1916-18 War Years	1950 Mrs M.Main	1976 E.Munro
1919 M.H.Benton	1951 Mrs M.Main	1977 E.Munro
1920 Mrs W.H.Nicolson	1952 M.Cameron	1978 E.Munro
1921 Mrs Crawford	1953 C.MacGeagh	1979 E.Rattray
1922 Mrs W.H.Nicolson	1954 Mrs M.Main	1980 E.Munro
1923 Mrs W.H.Nicolson	1955 B.Chetham	1981 E.Munro
1924 Mrs Buchanan	1956 B.Chetham	1982 E.Munro
1925 M.H.Benton	1957 Mrs Markes	1983 M.Ritchie
1926 H.C.Cameron	1958 Mrs M.Main	1984 E.J.Jack
1927 K.S.Macdonald	1959 E.Miller-Stirling	1985 E.Munro
1928 H.C.Cameron	1960 Mrs M.Main	1986 E.Munro
1929 H.C.Cameron	1961 Mrs Markes	1987 E.Munro
1930 K.S.Macdonald	1962 Mrs M.Main	1988 B.Hendry

The Leechman Cup

C.A.Leechman presented this silver cup on 5th November 1907 to the Moray Ladies' Golf Club to be played for annually by matchplay under handicap. This gesture prompted the Council to procure a case to be placed in the clubhouse for holding the club cups and to have them insured.

1908 Mrs Collis	1935 M.Drysdale	1964 Miss Paterson
1909 Elma Stuart	1936 Miss Webster	1965 J.M.McConachie
1910 Helen McIsaac	1937 Mrs C.Humble	1966 E.Geddes
1911 Helen McIsaac	1938 A.Anderson	1967 E.Geddes
1912 Mrs Collis	1939 Mrs Orr-Deas	1968 Mrs W.Souter
1913 Helen McIsaac	1940 M.Stephen	1969 E.Geddes
1914 A.E.Thomson	1941-45 War Years	1970 E.Geddes
1915 Isobel T.Hay	1946 Miss Wiseman	1971 E.Geddes
1916-18 War Years	1947 Mrs H.R.Spence	1972 E.Geddes
1919 Miss Webster	1948 C.MacGeagh	1973 S.Fraser-Moodie
1920 Miss Sellar	1949 Mrs M.Main	1974 Mrs E.Rattray
1921 Mrs Nicolson	1950 Mrs Christie	1975 Mrs B.Cramb
1922 Mrs Nicolson	1951 Miss B.Chetham	1976 Mrs J.Treloar
1923 Mrs W.Christie	1952 Mrs W.Christie	1977 Mrs E.Saul
1924 H.C.Cameron	1953 Miss B.Chetham	1978 Mrs G.Gormley
1925 Mrs Buchanan	1954 Miss M.Cameron	1979 Mrs E.Rattray
1926 M.Johnston	1955 Mrs Hamilton	1980 Mrs G.Gormley
1927 H.C.Cameron	1956 Mrs J.Lindsay	1981 Mrs G.Gormley
1928 Margot Cox	1957 Mrs J.R.Smith	1982 Mrs G.Gormley
1929 Mrs Ian Laing	1958 Miss B.Chetham	1983 Mrs E.Munro
1930 Miss M.Cox	1959 E.Miller-Stirling	1984 Miss E.J.Jack
1931 M.Drysdale	1960 E.Miller-Stirling	1985 Mrs M.Taylor
1932 H.E.Tomes	1961 Miss Allan	1986 Mrs A.Souter
1933 H.E.Tomes	1962 B.Chetham	1987 Mrs A.Cowper
1934 H.E.Tomes	1963 Mrs Mackay	1988 Mrs B.Hendry

The Mary Benton Quaich

The trophy was presented by Miss Mary Benton in 1949. The Benton family had a long connection with India and Lossiemouth and Mary Benton played to a single figure handicap at Moray for over thirty years.

1949 Mrs W.Christie	1963 C.MacGeagh	1976 Mrs M.Grant
1950 B.Chetham	1964 E.Miller-Stirling	1977 Mrs E.Munro
1951 M.Cameron	1965 E.Miller-Stirling	1978 Mrs S.Garrow
1952 Mrs Cumming	1966 C.MacGeagh	1979 I.Campbell
1953 Mrs Buchanan	1967 Miss E.Geddes	1980 Mrs E.Munro
1954 C.MacGeagh	1968 Miss E.Geddes	1981 Mrs E.Munro
1955 Mrs J.Buchanan	1969 J.M.McConachie	1982 Mrs M.Grant
1956 B.Chetham	1970 B.Malcolmson	1983 Mrs A.Cowper
1957 Mrs Wigram	1971 C.MacGeagh	1984 Mrs Ann Laing
1958 E.MacIntosh	1972 Mrs I.Douglas	1985 Mrs M.Taylor
1959 C.MacGeagh	1973 Mrs M.McIntosh	1986 Mrs M.Smith
1960 Mrs E.Saul	1974 B.Malcolmson	1987 Mrs M.Thirwell
1961 Mrs E.Saul	1975 G.Robertson	1988 Mrs B.Hendry
1962 Miss Paterson		

The Hilda Cameron Cup

The cup was presented by Mrs Hilda Cameron Marr in 1959 for foursomes matchplay under handicap, although it was played as singles from 1965-69. Hilda Cameron, the daughter of R.Innes Cameron, will long be remembered as the Moray golfer who acquitted herself with such distinction in the Scottish Ladies' Amateur Championship without having the good fortune to win it.

1959 Mrs Manchett & Mrs Saul	1974 Mrs D.Gordon & Mrs Saul
1960 Mrs Thomson & Mrs Hamilton	1975 Mrs Cramb & Mrs Treloar
1961 Mrs Clark & Mrs Douglas	1976 E.Rattray & I.Henderson
1962 Mrs Gordon & Mrs Thomson	1977 E.Rattray & Mrs A.Torr
1963 Miss Allan & Miss Anderson	1978 Mrs D.Gordon & Mrs Grant
1964 Mrs Saul & Mrs Thomson	1979 Mrs Gormley & K.Simpson
1965 Mrs M.Main	1980 Mrs E.Saul & Esther Jack
1966 Mrs Wadham	1981 Mrs E.Munro & Mrs Grant
1967 Mrs E.Saul	1982 Mrs Munro & Mrs M.Grant
1968 Mrs E.Saul	1983 I.Campbell & M.Thomson
1969 Mrs E.Saul	1984 I.Campbell & Mrs E.Smith
1970 Mrs Smith & Mrs Saul	1985 M.Grant & Mrs E.Rattray
1971 Mrs Smith & Mrs Saul	1986 E.Rattray & Mrs M.Smith
1972 I.Henderson & E.Rattray	1987 E.Rattray & Mrs H.Hepburn
1973 I.Henderson & E.Rattray	1988 B.Hendry & Mrs M.Thomson

The Ladies Gold Medal

The medal is enclosed in a shield with the heading — "Moray Ladies' Golf Club 1899". The shield states that the origin is unknown and that it was first played for in June 1949. This establishes the date of formation of the Moray Ladies' Golf Club in the last century.

1949 Mrs M.Main	1963 Miss McCombe	1976 Mrs E.Munro
1950 Miss C.MacGeagh	1964 Miss Paterson	1977 Mrs E.Munro
1951 Mrs M.Main	1965 Mrs M.Main	1978 Mrs E.Munro
1952 Mrs M.Main	1966 Miss MacGeagh	1979 Mrs E.Rattray
1953 Miss C.MacGeagh	1967 Mrs I.Douglas	1980 Mrs E.Munro
1954 Mrs M.Main	1968 Mrs M.Main	1981 Mrs E.Munro
1955 Mrs M.Main	1969 Mrs M.Main	1982 Mrs E.Munro
1956 Mrs M.Main	1970 Mrs Oulton	1983 Mrs E.Munro
1957 Mrs M.Main	1971 Miss MacGeagh	1984 Miss E.J.Jack
1958 Miss Chetham	1972 Miss MacGeagh	1985 Mrs B.Hendry
1959 Miss Chetham	1973 Miss Geddes	1986 Mrs E.Munro
1960 Miss C.MacGeagh	1974 Mrs J.R.Smith	1987 Mrs E.Munro
1961 Mrs M.Main	1975 Mrs B.Cramb	1988 Mrs J.Smith
1962 Mrs M.Main		

The G.S.Gault Trophy

The shield, for the annual winner of the low handicap section of the monthly medal competition, was presented by George Gault, a very popular and hard-working secretary from May 1974 until December 1982.

1983 W.A.Smith   1985 C.J.MacLeod   1987 C.J.MacLeod
1984 N.S.Grant   1986 K.G.Armit   1988 N.S.Grant

The Arcadia Trophy

This cup was presented in memory of the crew of the M.B.Arcadia who were lost at sea.

1984 D.J.Flett   1986 E.J.MacLeod   1988 D.A.Terron
1985 W.J.Stephen   1987 I.McGarva

The Boys Challenge Bowl

The presentation of this trophy, first played for in 1924, is not mentioned in the minutes. The Council of the day was undoubtedly distracted by the building of the third and last clubhouse and by the proposal for the reinstatement of Ramsay MacDonald, by then the Prime Minister of Great Britain.

1924 John A.Cattell	1949 Ian Rodger	1969 J.Baillie
1925 Ian McCulloch	1950 Ian Rodger	1970 M.Wilson
1926 A.Thorne	1951 W.F.Thomson	1971 F.N.Ralph
1927 Hamish West	1952 J.C.Thomson	1972 I.Imray
1928 W.Foster Gray	1953 W.Thomson	1973 D.J.Scott
1929 W.Foster Gray	1954 A.Thomson	1974 G.R.King
1930 J.S.Maclean	1955 A.Thomson	1975 J.Smith
1931 R.West	1956 A.Thomson	1976 M.C.Page
1932 W.Mackie	1957 George Smith	1977 J.B.Thomson
1933 S.Harris	1958 George Smith	1978 S.Mitchell
1934 R.D.M.Batchelor	1959 D.Strachan	1979 B.J.Smith
1935 W.D.Campbell	1960 R.D.Morrison	1981 G.D.Smith
1936 John Halliday	1961 R.D.Morrison	1982 G.D.Smith
1937 J.P.Henderson	1962 N.A.McConachie	1983 J.W.Souter
1938 Thomas Marr	1963 J.M.McKenzie	1984 A.J.Smith
1939 T.C.K.Marr	1964 J.M.McKenzie	1985 A.J.Smith
1940-45 War Years	1965 M.J.M.Tulloch	1986 K.Thomson
1946 Mitchell Campbell	1966 M.J.M.Tulloch	1987 K.Thomson
1947 G.D.Anderson	1967 S.Thomson	1988 B.M.Rattray
1948 G.D.Anderson	1968 N.Masson	

The Margetts Cup

The cup was given to the junior boys' section in 1953 by Farquhar Thomson. It was presented to him by Pat Margetts, who was a Galway jeweller.

1953 C.J.MacLeod	1964 G.Farquhar	1975 S.Mitchell
1954 John C.Thomson	1965 J.Brown	1976 A.B.Cave
1955 K.Tait	1966 M.Wilson	1979 B.J.Smith
1956 R.D.Morrison	1967 M.J.M.Tulloch	1981 W.I.Watson
1957 R.D.Morrison	1968 A.Gordon	1982 K.Thomson
1958 D.J.Strachan	1969 I.Imray	1983 B.M.Rattray
1959 N.A.McConachie	1970 D.Edwards	1984 A.J.Smith
1960 D.Slater	1971 D.Edwards	1985 M.Young
1961 D.Slater	1972 G.R.King	1986 K.Thomson
1962 R.D.Morrison	1973 W.Duncan	1987 G.Muir
1963 S.Thomson	1974 M.Macleman	1988 S.Sharp

BIBLIOGRAPHY

Letters on Golf. BY A PARISH MINISTER. (Elgin 1889)

The Records of Elgin 1234-1800. CRAMOND. (Aberdeen 1908)

Elgin Past and Present. H.B. MACKINTOSH. (Elgin 1914)

Quick Cuts To Good Golf. STANCLIFFE. (London 1920)

Out of the Rough. BERNARD DARWIN. (London 1932)

The Life of James Ramsay MacDonald. LORD ELTON. (London 1939)

Teach Yourself Golf. J.C. JESSOP. (London 1950)

The Bobby Jones Story. GRANTLAND RICE. (London 1954)

Golf Is My Game. BOBBY JONES. (London 1959)

Spinners Yarn. I.A.R. PEEBLES. (London 1977)

The (Ab)use of Power. JAMES MARGACH. (London 1978)

Personal Memories of Royal Dornoch Golf Club. DONALD GRANT. (1978)

Ramsay MacDonald. DAVID MARQUAND. (London 1978)

Golf in the Making. I.T. HENDERSON AND D.I. STIRK. (Crawley 1979)

Royal Aberdeen Golf Club. 200 YEARS OF GOLF. (Aberdeen 1980)

Good Golf Guide to Scotland. DAVID HAMILTON. (Edinburgh 1982)

The Elgin Club. LEONARD F. IVALL. (Elgin 1984)

Early Aberdeen Golf. DAVID HAMILTON. (Glasgow 1985)

Golf. The History of an Obsession. DAVID STIRK. (Oxford 1987)

The District of Moray. CHARLES McKEAN. (Edinburgh 1987)

Forgotten General. DONALD LINDSAY. (Salisbury 1987)

INDEX

References to Lossiemouth and the Moray Golf Club are not indexed nor are names appearing only in the Appendix.